GABRIEL ABRAHAM SINGBEH

SOLD OUT

[A TRUE STORY]

PRESERVED FOR GOD'S PURPOSES
IN TORTURE, TRAFFICKING AND TERROR

SOLD OUT MINISTRIES
Port Orchard, Washington

SOLD OUT:
Preserved for God's Purposes
in Torture, Trafficking, and Terror

by Gabriel Abraham Singbeh

Copyright © 2021

Published by
Sold Out Ministries

ISBN 978-0-578-96336-5

Unless otherwise noted, all scripture is from
the King James Version of the Bible.

SOLD OUT MINISTRIES
Calvary Church of Port Orchard
810 SW Wildwood Rd
Port Orchard, WA 98367

www.SoldOutServant.net

Cover and Interior Design by Mark Dinsmore
MD Creative / MarkDinsmoreDesign.com

Cover photo: Shutterstock

PRINTED IN THE UNITED STATES OF AMERICA

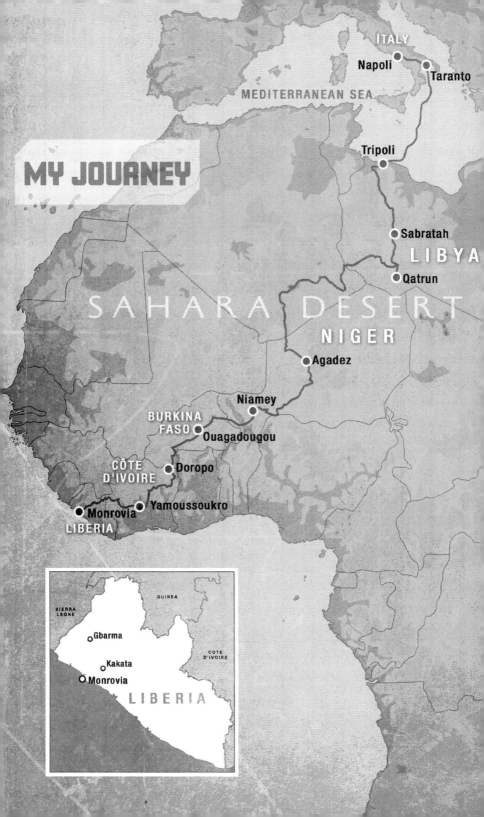

MY JOURNEY

ITALY
Napoli
Taranto

MEDITERRANEAN SEA

Tripoli

Sabratah

LIBYA

Qatrun

SAHARA DESERT

NIGER

Agadez

Niamey

BURKINA FASO
Ouagadougou

CÔTE D'IVOIRE
Doropo

Yamoussoukro

Monrovia
LIBERIA

SIERRA LEONE

GUINEA

Gbarma

Kakata

Monrovia

CÔTE D'IVOIRE

LIBERIA

PRODUCTION NOTE

In the process of editing and formatting this gripping personal account, the booksmith could not help noticing parallels between Gabriel Abraham's experience and the travails of Paul the Apostle.

Thus, the chapter titles and headings were inspired by Pauls' second letter to the Corinthian Church, written about A.D. 56, where the apostle recounts how he was

> *In journeyings often, in perils of waters, in perils of robbers, in perils by mine own countrymen, in perils by the heathen, in perils in the city, in perils in the wilderness, in perils in the sea, in perils among false brethren; In weariness and painfulness, in watchings often, in hunger and thirst, in fastings often, in cold and nakedness. Beside those things that are without, that which cometh upon me daily, the care of all the churches.*
>
> — 2 Corinthians 11:26-28

As Paul also declared, "For our light affliction, which is but for a moment, is working for us a far more exceeding and eternal weight of glory" (2 Cor. 4:17). In the case of Gabriel Abraham Singbeh, it already has. May every reader be challenged and inspired to similarly declare,

> *I entrust my spirit into your hand. Rescue me, LORD, for you are a faithful God.*
>
> —Psalm 31:5

CONTENTS

FOREWORD

JANE ALBRIGHT

It was one of those moments—infrequent, but clear and unmistakable. When the Holy Spirit speaks to me in such a tangible way that I almost hear His voice. Glancing around me at this small Baptist church I had just started attending in Naples, Italy, I noticed a striking, young African man sitting alone just across the aisle from me.

This was not unusual—this church had a number of African congregants. But there was something about him that drew me to him, I could not stop noticing him. I estimated him to be in his mid-twenties. He had serious, sad eyes. We struck up a conversation, and I learned he had just turned eighteen. He wanted an education, but right now he desperately needed a job. Speaking with the pastor, I learned he had just recently moved to the area, owned almost nothing, and was staying with someone on a temporary basis. He vouched that he was a sincere believer with real needs. Both the pastor and his wife encouraged me to help him out if the Lord was leading me to do so.

As I came to learn more about Abraham's situation, I was compelled to act (Isaiah 30:21). We became attached to each other very quickly, and I knew I was supposed to take him into my home during this season of our lives. The Lord had provided me a well-paying job with the US Navy at the base in Naples, with a housing allowance. How could I not offer up one of my four bedrooms to a fellow believer who had none?

Thus, I acquired a second son, an African one at that, and Abraham acquired a second mom. This was not on my list of things to do during my overseas job tour. Over my computer in Naples, I posted a sign that said, "The Lord calls us to positions we never applied for."

As I came to know Abraham during the two years he lived with me, I continued to be amazed at the work of God's grace in his life. His spiritual insight, faith, and devotion to Jesus was unlike anything you see in most Americans, young or old.

During our time together, I learned some of what you are about to read but did not know the entire account until he wrote this one. While I and others had been urging him to put his story in writing, it has taken some time for him to overcome his reluctance to re-live these events. You will soon understand why.

I am grateful to God for His giving me a small part to play in the amazing life of this amazing young man. As Abraham would say, "To God be the glory!"

Jane Albright (a.k.a. "Mom")

July 2021

My parents' house
under construction

My Mother and
Father

THE JOURNEY BEGINS

MONROVIA, LIBERIA

On a cold Friday morning at about 12:15 a.m., the Lord in His infinite love and mercy granted that a child be born into this world and a member added to the Singbeh family. This child, like every other, will grow up knowing one important truth—that there is a God Who created him and this world. Without this God, Who is the Lord Jesus Christ, he cannot do anything or become who he wants to be.

My name is Gabriel Abraham Singbeh. I was born in Liberia unto Mr. and Mrs. Bennito Singbeh in the year of 1999, December 24. I have five sisters and a brother. I am the third-born in my family, the second and last boy child. I was born in Monrovia, the capital city of Liberia in West Africa. Monrovia is located on the Atlantic Coast at Cape Montserrado, one of the 15 counties of Liberia. The largest city in Liberia, Monrovia has a population of about one million.

Being born in Monrovia city is a source of pride for many Liberians. Being a "city boy" (or girl) is something most Liberians take very seriously. However, being born in this city wasn't something I could take pride in because from my birth to age 15, my life had had many ups and downs. My birth, as told by my mom, was not a pleasant one, and my twin brother did not survive. My mother told me many times about this difficult birth, and no one was sure if she was going to survive either because of what she went through. But as God lives, He made it possible, and today she still breathes the breath of life.

In many tribes in Liberia, especially the Kpell tribe, which I am from, there is a belief that when a mother dies or nearly dies in giving birth and the child lives, that child is considered evil or cursed. The parent or the child itself must be taken from the community before they cause the same effect in other families. My mother of course got sick, and so the elders of our community told my dad to leave. So my dad took us to his home village of Gbarma located in Todee District of Montserrado County, where I spent half of my early life.

GBARMA, LIBERIA

Growing up in the village was challenging because my father was not working. He had planned to return to his job with a construction company in the city after moving to Gbarma, but my mom was so sick, he had to stay home to take care of her, me, and my older brother and sister, who were still very young. So he lost his job.

According to mom, who always told me about events that transpired when I was little, my father then decided to start farming in order to support the family. His dream of becoming a construction engineer was interrupted because he would not see his family suffer. He had once worked as a soldier for the local government before I was even born, but during Liberia's 14-year civil war, he lost his father and three older brothers. Unhappy and frustrated, he retired from the military after the new government took over.

My mother never had the opportunity to go to school. All income came through the jobs my father was able to get. Mom and Dad told me many things that happened during the time I was born, but what caught my attention was how many struggles they had and how much they suffered. They did everything they could to give me and my brother and sisters a better life but failed because of the society in which they live.

My dad's decision to move to his home village was not his fault—the rules of our society and cultural superstitions has had a great effect on my family, including me, till this day, even after 20 years. We still live below the poverty line with nothing to show for my parents' many years of hard work and no good foundation for me and my siblings.

Have you ever been in a situation where things at first look good, but later change and almost everything you do or find yourself in seems to work against you? Do you or have you ever felt like all your plans, dreams, hopes, and desires are being shattered, and all you can see is blank space of nothing at all? Well if you have not, I would like you to know that these feelings are real, they do happen. The person now speaking to you is someone who has experienced many such moments.

Before I dive into telling you my story and how I made it this far, I would like to point out that it was all by the Lord Jesus' grace and protection that brought me to where I am now. Without God Almighty and our Lord Jesus Christ, I would not have survived. As the Scripture says in Zechariah 4:6,

> *Then He answered and spake unto me, saying, "This is the word of the LORD unto Zerubbabel, saying, 'Not by might, nor by power, but by my spirit,' saith the LORD of hosts."*

It has all been by the grace of God that I have made it this far to be where I am now! This is why I find it pleasing to share with you what He has done in my life from birth until today.

Growing up in my village was not easy. There were beautiful moments, and there were bad ones as well. No good family wants to see their children live an unhealthy or poor life that deprives them of the freedom to do things or get what they need or desire. My family was the same, mostly my mom, who loved me so dearly.

I suffered a lot of health issues when I was a child. I could not walk or talk well for a long time. According to my mom, they took me to many physicians, some of them native doctors. Like the woman with the issue of blood in the Bible (Mark 5:25-34), my parents spent most of the little money they had from their farm to help me get well, but nothing worked. My father came to believe that I was indeed a curse and an evil child who brought them suffering because everything changed for them the moment I was born.

My father could not continue anymore. He had given up on me, and of course I will not blame him for that, he did try his best. I do not know what I would have done if it were me. My dad decided to leave me with his mother, who also lived in the village at the time, and move the rest of the family to the city of Kakata. My mother did not give up on me, but because Dad was the man of the home and a husband to her, she needed to obey his decision to leave me in the village and move to Kakata. But Grandma was not able to care for me, and so she sent me to a nearby church with a home that took care of disabled people and children with health problems.

I was at the church for about two years and nine months before I learned to walk. By the time I started talking, I was already five years of age according to my dad. During the time Mom and Dad were in Kakata, they begat another two children, and these were Famata, second to me, and Sarah, third to me, who is the fifth-born of my siblings.

When my parents heard that I was now walking and able to talk, they decided to come back for me. For them, this was a great miracle and meant that God had some sort of big plan for me on earth. It took me time to know that my dad and mom were my real parents because they had left me for many years, and I had only known my grandmother and those who took care of me at the church. I can still remember, when my mother saw me walking and talking, she burst into tears. Not knowing her that well, I asked myself, "Why is this woman crying?"

My dad came and took me by the hands, hugged me, and shed tears a little—of course he is a man and men are not to show their tears much as it reveals their weakness—but my dad did it anyway. He could not hold in the tears as emotions took over. Upon taking me by the hand and hugging me, he quickly lifted me up and the only words I could hear were, "I am sorry, son!"

In my mind, I was like, "Why is he telling me sorry? Did he do anything wrong to me, or did he hurt someone that I love?" Right away, I thought of Grandma. But I guess the simple answer to these questions is that he should not have left me no matter what, I was his child.

When my parents came back to the village for me, they decided it was time my father take another

farm job because his job in Kakata was not paying
him well. In fact, his boss would not pay him for up
to two or three months at a time. So my dad decided
he would stay in the village and continue his farm
work.

When I mention farming, you might be thinking
of modern farming where one uses machines to
cultivate the land and plant the crops. I would like
to take your thoughts off such. Because the kind of
farming I am talking about is poor-man's farming,
where all the work is done by hand, not machines.
My dad never had enough money to purchase
machines. Even if he wanted to, it would take him
five or six years of constant farming before he could
afford one because the farms were not large.

Preparing, planting, and growing crops in Liberia is
a very long process that takes four to six months of
hard work every year. This is the type of farming I
knew growing up, which is very different than other
countries.

TRAIN UP A CHILD

As far back as I can remember, my mother talked about God and prayed with me every day. She told me how much God loved me, that I could trust Him no matter what, and that He had a special purpose for my life. At age six, when I started talking very well, my mom began taking me to her local church in the village, The Christ Will Christian Fellowship Church, where they often preached and taught in our local dialect, which I am really not good at speaking and, as you know, I had speech problems.

However, as mom saw my love and passion for wanting to know God and his Word, she started teaching me some of my favorite Bible verses like Psalm 34:11, which reads "Come, ye children, hearken unto me: I will teach you the fear of the LORD," and Proverbs 3:6, which says "Trust in the LORD with all thine heart; and lean not unto thine own understanding. In all thy ways acknowledge him, and he shall direct thy paths."

She also taught me many Bible stories. Among these, my favorites were the story of Joseph who was sold by his brethren picturing Christ's betrayal, and the story of David and Goliath, which shows how, with trust and faith in God, we can overcome the fear of our enemies and defeat them with the help of God, no matter how big they are.

I was talking well now but could not read at all, and I was not in school. But my mother, who could not read well herself, saw that I needed to learn the Bible and how to apply it to my life. I began to wonder why she felt so strongly that her children needed God's Word in our lives. I would listen to my mom as she talked to me in her native dialect with our little poor oil lantern on. She would go on telling me about how amazing, big, and good God is and how that He is everyone's Father, no matter the earthly fathers we have.

I once asked my mom how she came to know the Lord Jesus and why she so much loved talking about God and reading His Word, and she told me that she came to know the Lord Jesus Christ as her Lord and Savior at a much later age. According to her, she grew up in a family who really didn't believe in God.

Their beliefs were in the worship of little household idols and witchcraft practices. Mom told me that when she was very young, on multiple occasions, her grandmother, that is, her mother's mother, tried to introduce her to their idols and witchcraft practices. But her dad refused, even though he was not a saved Christian at the time.

Because of the constant troubles my mom's father got from his mother-in-law and other family members over his refusal to initiate his daughter (my mom) into their beliefs and worship, he decided to move his family to Monrovia, the capital city, where my mother later met my dad and also accepted the Lord Jesus Christ as her Lord and personal Savior in the Assemblies of God Church at age 28. Since then, she has seen the Lord do so many great and wonderful things in her life as she continued to serve Him. That is why she found it right to teach me and my siblings about God and His Word, the Bible.

Sometimes I would ask her the question that almost everyone asks at some point. I would say, "Mama, if God is so good, amazing, kind, and everyone's Father, why is he allowing us to suffer? Why did he allow me to be sick? Why did he allow my twin brother to die, and why did he bring me on earth in the first place if he knew I was going to suffer and not walk nor talk until age five?"

Most times, the only thing she would say is that God loves me as his child and he has a reason for everything and that I can trust Him no matter the situation because He is good and faithful to deliver me from anything, like He did by allowing me to talk and walk. As my mom repeated these things to me, it made me want to know Jesus better. But even at that, I still had lots of questions and doubts in my head because of the continual suffering my family and I experienced.

IN HUNGER AND THIRST

Living in the village was not pleasant at all. We barely had enough food to eat. My family has lived their whole lives without savings or a bank account, and my brother and sisters and I were out of school.

In the village, there was no electricity, no roads for cars, and no safe drinking water. We normally got our drinking water from the stream, and if the stream went dry during the dry season, we walked about three miles with buckets to get water for drinking and cooking.

As for food, even a grain of rice is as valuable as a diamond. To buy food, we normally process palm oil, put it into a 4- to 5-gallon container, put it on our head, and walk about four hours' distance to sell it in the market. We then buy food with the money, leaving us sometimes with no money left over.

The food we get from the market must last two weeks, because market is open only every two weeks. So we also ate bush food such as cassava, plantains, eddoes, and yams, and we normally had only one meal a day, in the evening. I can still remember how my sisters and I would come close with our spoon in our hands when our mother was dishing up the food. We would be singing all those childish songs that sometimes have no meaning, with the goal of getting our mom to put more food in our bowls.

After eating, about 8 p.m., everyone would already be inside their houses because the village is surrounded with bushes, and darkness falls early. The moonlight was the only source of light we had at night. As most people long for summer, that is how we longed for the moonlight during the dry season.

During this amazing time of the year, the children get to play outside at night under the moonlight, and our parents get to visit with their neighbors and friends whom they have not had the chance to meet due to farming work.

My uncle's house in Monrovia

My school in Monrovia

IN PERILS BY MINE OWN COUNTRYMEN

KAKATA

I was nine years old before I saw anything powered by electricity. This was when my parents sent me to live with my uncle in Kakata. Going to live with my uncle was very difficult for me. It was a moment I never thought would happen.

I missed my parents at once, especially my mother who is also my best friend. My uncle was someone who I never knew existed; he had never come to the village to visit us. But as my parents saw it as a good thing, and being only nine years old, I had no choice but to obey because a child's duty is to obey his parents. This new transition was difficult for me as it meant leaving all my friends and immediate family.

Living in the village was not easy, but it was my home. In the village, there were beautiful people and places that I cherished, such as the rainforest, the woods where the monkeys often came to play, the Du Rivers where we often swam during the dry season, and amazing people such as my grandmother who told me beautiful stories. But I had to let go of what I wanted and understand that this was what my parents wished, something they saw as good for me.

My mom had always told me that God had a great plan for me even though we had no idea what that plan was. But because of her strong faith in God for a better future, I got the courage to have faith and believe that things would get better, and that my moving to the city would help make that possible.

However, things do not always work out the way we plan or think they will. In my case, I was a village boy who knew nothing about city life nor the injustice and unfairness that life in the city can bring.

As we began the journey to Kakata, I was filled with confidence and hope—I thought, at least now I will have the chance to go to school and find a church where I will be taught the Bible more in-depth. I told myself that I will go to school, graduate, learn the Bible, and teach people about God's Word just as Mom had always told me.

I promised myself that I would be that good child that my mother had always wanted me to be by achieving my goal of helping them out of poverty. My dreams and desires took hold of me that I could think of nothing more than accomplishing them. I needed to stay focused, be respectful, kind, and patient, and endure. I thought that as long as I believed in God, my life would change spontaneously. All my plans and goals were set, even though I was young. And I thought my uncle would help me achieve these goals.

When I first went to live with my uncle and his family, everything was well. I was welcomed with an open hand and immediately put into school, the "Pentecostal Conqueror High School" in Margibi County, Kakata. With confidence and motivation, I also fully engaged in serving my local church in

Kakata. For the first two years things were great, and I was given every necessary attention and care as a young boy.

However, my uncle lost his job, and then everything changed. As the Scriptures make us to understand in Proverbs 16:9, "A man's heart deviseth his way: but the LORD directeth his steps."

My uncle, whom I thought would help me achieve my goals, was influenced by his wife, who now saw me as a threat to her own children's education and burden to their family because she was now providing for the home by herself. She had to pay both my school fees and her children's. She wanted to send me back to the village to my parents.

My uncle opposed sending me back to the village because I was his sister's son, and he had promised that he would take care of me no matter what. So they decided to move to Monrovia in search of work for him. We settled in Bushrod Island Clara Town in Monrovia, and things became even worse for me. My uncle still could not find work, so I was no longer in school or able to go to church regularly.

From being a child that was loved and taken care of by my uncle's family, I became like a house slave doing all the chores while their children went to school. Many times, I asked myself why things were happening the way they were. I became afraid, lonely, and cried many times because I was now far from my mom and dad and did not know my way back to the village.

I was nine years old when I left the village and had lived in Kakata for nearly three years without going to the village, nor did my parents ever come to visit me, which made me even more afraid and lonely. But they trusted my uncle so much and he always told them I was fine whenever he visited the village, so they never came to check on me.

I felt abandoned by my parents and God. All my dreams, motivation, and desires to help my family were now shattered, and I had no choice but to accept life as it was. I had to obey everything my uncle's wife told me to do in the house. School was no longer an option. Going to church and studying the Bible as I used to in Kakata all stopped. I did not understand what all this meant—whether it was God's will that I pass through this suffering or if I was being punished for something I did wrong, I had no idea.

Making matters worse, my uncle, who I had hoped, as the head of the home, would talk to his wife, could not help. His joblessness and other frustrations led him to start drinking. He soon became an alcoholic, and this became another major problem in the home.

Uncle's inability to provide for the home was another event that made me wonder why God would allow such a thing to happen. I had already seen that my father's inability to find steady work meant that we lived in poverty. I became greatly concerned as I watched these events transpire within my uncle's family. I many times wondered if this was all my fault because it happened to my father after I was born, and now that I am living with my uncle, it is happening to him. I got so afraid that my uncle might give up on me like my father once did, when he left me behind and moved to Kakata. My uncle might do the same.

My uncle's wife resented me and considered me an outsider because I was not part of her immediate family. My uncle, on other hand, did not show any sign of resentment toward me, but he never tried to help solve the problem either. His idea of dealing with the problems in his home was to drink alcohol to forget them. He would go out during the day to search for a job but would return home drunk. I would sometimes be the one to help get him water to take a shower and advise him to take a good and right path, even though I had my own struggles and worries. As his drunkenness continued, he lost the respect of his wife and their two children, Moses and Alice. For me, I had to respect him because he was my uncle and the only family person I had and knew in Monrovia.

IN FASTINGS OFTEN

I began looking for place where I could have peace. My world was turned upside down, and I had no

hope of seeing my parents again or going to school.
I started fasting and praying as my mom used to do,
with the belief that God would open doors for me
to leave my uncle's house and find someone who
would take me to my parents in the village.

As I began this time of personal fasting and prayers,
I decided to find a new church of my own. We
had been in Monrovia nearly a year, but we did
not have a specific church for worship. My uncle
was a Catholic, and his wife and children were
Pentecostals but she would not take me to church
with them because I had to stay home to clean and
watch over the house. Not going to church grieved
my heart because my mom always took me to
church.

As I watched them go their separate ways on
Sundays, I would sometimes escape out of the
house and go to one of my community friends'
church. When my uncle realized I was leaving the
house to attend church on Sundays, he decided to
take me to church with him. I was very happy about
this at first. But as I carefully observed their way of

worship and doctrine, I just could not fit in. I told him that I would like to find my own church, and he agreed, which led me to attending the James R. Davies Memorial Baptist Church located in Freeport community, Bushrod Island, Monrovia, Liberia.

James R. Davis Memorial Baptist Church

As I began going to church and engaging into church activities again, I finally started finding my true purpose and meaning to life. My newly found church was hosting a four-day revival service with a guest preacher from the United States of America.

I did not know about the revival, as my uncle's wife gave me so many household tasks, I had no time to go to church during the week. However, my friend Michael Myers told me about the services. It was the last day, so I left everything and hurried the four miles to church.

I was already late, and the guest preacher was almost finished preaching. Standing outside the main entrance of the church door within the corridor, I still was touched by the last few words I heard from the pulpit. During the altar call, the preacher kept saying, "There is someone here today going through a life without peace, happiness, or joy and feeling left alone and lonely. But today, Jesus is calling you. He wants to change that for you and give you His peace. Come as you are, come as you are."

It felt like the preacher was talking directly to me.

As these words took hold of my heart, I also heard a voice speaking within my heart. I believe this was the Holy Spirt, even though I did not understand it at the time. This smooth gentle little voice I heard kept saying that "It is time to make things right." I did not know what that meant, but being touched by both the preacher's words and the voice that spoke to my heart, there was nothing I could think of that moment but to give my life to Christ. So, in 2012 at age 12, I gave my life to the Lord Jesus Christ.

It was a cool Thursday evening, a day that I will never forget. The memory of it will last with me until the day the Lord calls me home. Accepting the Lord Jesus that day changed my life in dramatic ways. It was a day that I felt a sense of relief and freedom. I found my true purpose in life as a child of God and someone who was created to serve, teach, and preach the gospel message of Christ. I could not keep it to myself. Instead, I went on telling everyone that I met in my community, mostly my young teen friends.

But for my uncle's wife, that day meant I was disobedient in not completing the house chores she had instructed me to do. Thus, I was punished with a beating and denied food for a day. I gave my life to Christ thinking everything was going to change for the better, and it became even worse. His wife constantly reminded my uncle that I was not her child; that my family was in the village; and the village was where I belonged.

I suffered many things from my uncle's wife, but one thing was against everything most important to me. She said I had to stop going to services on Sunday and instead do her work and watch over the house. I had told myself and promised God that I would always be in His house on Sunday to worship with my fellow believers. Preventing me from going to church meant taking everything I loved away from me. Only at church did I experience the love of others.

I tried to explain the situation to my uncle, but he did nothing about it. However, I decided one evening to ask her to please allow me to go to church and worship on Sundays. Upon hearing this, she became very upset and slapped me in the face. She told me that I had to make a decision: either obey her orders and still live under her roof or, if I insisted on going to church on Sundays, to leave her house.

I again asked my uncle to talk to his wife or take me back to my family in the village. He said it was not worth going back to the village and that if I wanted to go, then I should go by myself. He knew I had not been to the village for years now and did not know my way back.

DESPISED AND REJECTED

The situation continued to worsen. Once, my uncle left for a month to visit his sick brother in the hospital in Gand Bassa County. My uncle's wife had discovered that I had been going to church on Sunday when she and her children were not home and took advantage of my uncle's absence to put me out of the house. I begged her and cried on her, but she would not allow me to stay. As it happened, I ended up sleeping in the street and in old cars. For about a month after my uncle's return, he did not bother to look for me. His wife had told him that I had decided to return to my parents in the village, which of course was a lie.

I was homeless for about nine months. I did not attend church during this time because I was homeless and without any good clothes. After several months, my friend Michael finally went to my uncle's home to ask about me and was told that I had gone to the village to visit my family. Eventually, Michael discovered that I was still in Monrovia and homeless. He found me, took me in, and had me do some clothes-selling for him. I was now able to start paying my own school fees at the PAYGMA high school. However, I had to drop out of school again due to the collapse of Michael's business and his travel to Ghana to visit his mom. But I had learned how to sell, and local small business owners let me sell their goods so I could buy food to eat.

I was now somewhat far away from the James R. Davies Memorial Baptist Church, so I visited other nearby churches and began holding my own community Bible studies. It was now 2013, and during this time, I met a pastor who also lived in Doe Community. As Pastor Elisha watched me teach during one of our community Bible Studies, he became interested in knowing me better. We became friends, and he even invited me to preach in one of his Sunday services.

As our friendship grew, Pastor Elisha began to ask me about my family and what I was doing to make a living. I explained my situation and all that had happened. He was touched and asked me if I was willing to trace the route to my home village. According to Pastor Elisha, he once had a brother in a town close to my village. I immediately responded that I would like to, and we agreed that he would help me find my family.

REUNITED!

I became very excited to see my family again. Our trip was delayed for three months because Pastor Elisha got sick, but once he recovered, we were able to go and see my family. It was a moment of great joy for me and my family. We hugged each other and shed tears and many more good things happened that day. My parents had been fooled and lied to by my uncle, making them to believe that all was well with me for all the years that I was way from home.

Returning to the village was strange; almost everything looked different. My dad had built another little house in the village, made very large sugarcane, corn, and rice farms, and another two sisters had been born into our family, making us a total of seven children—five girls and two boys.

Upon seeing my beloved mother after so many years, her first question was, "Son, are you still serving the Lord? Is your faith still strong in the Lord?" Upon hearing that I was a born-again child of God, she got so excited and happy that I could see the joy in her deep smiles.

As for Dad, since he barely talked about biblical or spiritual matters, his question was what was I planning on doing after high school. I was only 14 years old then, so he could not directly ask the question, "What job are you doing now?!"

I was able to spend three days with my family. We had some beautiful moments during those three days, and it felt so wonderful and refreshing. Seeing my family again gave me courage to keep pressing on in faith and trust in the Lord knowing that He is

God and can take care of me and give me a better future.

Leaving the village with Pastor Elisha on the fourth day, I was again full of confidence and motivation. I began considering all the plans and goals I had set at age nine before going to live with my uncle. I began having an even more clear picture of what God really wanted me to be and to do. I became even more convinced that it was my calling to serve God. He had already started using me at an early age.

After my friend Michael found me in the street, he clothed me and gave me shelter and the means to earn money for my school fees. I realized that God still had a plan for me as Mom had always said, and I felt there was a need to serve Him in every way possible and acceptable to Him. Even though I always had this in mind, not seeing my parents for so long was one thing that just could not leave my head. I many times cried and asked God why, but when I saw my family again, it all became clear that God had been working things out all along—I just couldn't see it at first.

"THE LORD ADDED TO THE CHURCH DAILY..."

Upon returning to Monrovia, I immediately restarted my small group Bible study and prayer meeting with the goal of bringing many souls unto Christ and His kingdom. Within three months, the small group of just 14 participants began growing. Soon we were approaching 40 persons, many of whom gave their lives to Christ.

I had started the group for youth only, but as we visited homes to have the Bible studies, adult family members in these homes began joining us. By the time we reached 65 persons, about 26 people had given their lives to Christ, and the homes we visited could not contain that many people. Additionally, I was only 14 years old (nearly 15), and not equipped to handle so many people.

Since my church, James R. Davis Memorial Baptist Church, was not far from many of the Bible study members' homes, I quietly contacted the church Evangelism Director, Rev. J. Henry Baysah, and he came to one of our meetings. Upon seeing the group, he was impressed and encouraged them to attend the church. Those who had gotten saved began attending the church, got baptized, and were added to the membership. Most of them are still in the church to this day, serving in different departments.

Under the leadership of Senior Pastor, Rev. G. Benjamin Stewart Yeanay Sr., I was given the opportunity to serve in several areas/departments within the church. I served as Secretary and chaplain in the Youth Department. At age 15, I was given the position of Sunday school teacher and preacher for the Children's Ministry. I was also part of the evangelism outreach, ministering to the sick in hospitals, such as the John F. Kennedy Hospital, the Redemption Hospital, and other local hospitals in the area. Sometimes we also visited the prison compound to minister to those in prison.

Rev. Yeanay eventually left for the U.S. to complete his studies, and Associate Pastor Rev. Boima G. Tarlah took over. There were many changes. Many people did not consider Rev. Tarlah fit or spiritual enough to take over such a large congregation, and members began leaving the church. Within the first six months of Tarlah's leadership, the church was left with only a small group of members.

Before Rev. Yeanay left, a member in the church was paying my school fees. But he was one of the ones that left the church, and I ended up dropping out of school again because there was no means to pay my fees. My friend Pastor Elisha was again very generous and promised to pay the rest of my tuition for that year. But something came up that prevented Pastor Elisha from helping me.

His cousin, whom he considered a brother, wanted him to move to Germany and continue his biblical studies from there. Pastor Elisha decided to go, and he needed to keep the money he had promised for my schooling to pay for this trip. I could not hold this against him because he was trying to help and of course, he had helped me previously by taking me to see my parents in the village.

Pastor Elisha's brother, by the name of Olsen, lived in Germany and told Elisha that he would help get him there, but that Elisha would have to travel to Niger first. From there, they would work out his visa process. Pastor Elisha decided he would take me along if I were willing. He encouraged me to come, saying that this would help bring my dreams and all I had been praying for into reality. I would have the opportunity to complete my high school and go to the Bible school of my choice.

Hearing this from someone who had always helped me out when I needed it and took me to see my parents—and not just that but talked about fulfilling my dreams—I became very excited. But at age 15, I did not want to leave my family. Although life so far had not been pleasant, my family, my country, and my church still meant a lot to me. I was not ready to leave them and travel to an unknown, faraway place that I had not been before nor any of my family members. I had been separated from them more than once and missed them so much.

As I evaluated things in my head, I told Elisha
that I was going to think about it more and would
have to inform my family. But as he saw this as an
opportunity for a brighter future for me, he decided
to go with me to meet with my parents and assure
them that he would take care of me. As I heard the
word "Take care of you," I was like, please not again!
My uncle said similar things to my mother and at the
end abandoned me.

I was scared and nearly told my mom to say no. But
Elisha had proved himself trustworthy by taking me
to see my parents and even helping me out in many
areas. So I was a little calm and waited to hear what
my parents had to say. Of course, they were very
good at giving me up. It had happened before, and I
was convinced that this time would be no different.

But I was wrong. My parents refused, at least the
first time. They wanted more proof from Elisha
and his brother in Germany that this travel was
legitimate. Until he provided proof, my parents
would not let him take me with him because this

was a distant land where none of them had been or lived before.

Upon hearing this from my family, Elisha and I had to go back to the city and see if he could provide proof that the travel he wanted us to do was legal. As we headed back to the city, I could see the disappointment on Elisha's face as he felt as one who was untrustworthy.

However, I could not blame my parents, they were doing their job as good parents. They had already made the mistake of sending me to live with Uncle, and that did not work out well. They did not want to repeat that mistake and so needed to take parental protective measures. I personally found their decision and request worthy because I was already worried about getting into another period of intense suffering, as it had been for most of my entire life.

With the look and mood I saw in Elisha when leaving the village that day, I felt that it was over. I thought he would not trouble his brother about getting a letter of proof or anything, since it was only him, Elisha, his brother had promised to bring to Germany, not two people.

But Elisha saw it as necessary to bring me along. So after three months, Elisha invited me to his house and told me he would like us to pay another visit to my family so he could talk to them again. I had already forgotten about this trip and so to bring it up again got me wondering what he really saw in me that made him want to take me with him to this far distant land.

I told him I was going to first visit the village and let my parents know that he is coming but as he insisted, I told him to give me at least a week or two to think about the matter. In the process, he had already contacted a friend who worked at the Ministry of Foreign Affairs in the passport department to prepare our passports and other official legal documents that we needed for traveling.

All this effort and help from Elisha led me to believe that he could be trusted. So we took another trip to the village, but this time Elisha had an invitation letter from his brother as well as the passports and other documents. He had been hiding his brother's letter from me; perhaps he wanted to surprise me by showing me how serious he was. After showing my parents the passports, other documents, and his brother's letter, my parents agreed to let Elisha take me along with him. We then returned to Monrovia to prepare for the journey.

PREPARING TO LEAVE

In early October 2015, after two months of preparation, praying, fasting, and seeking God for His protection and guidance and with blessing from my family, we embarked on our journey for Niger which was said to be the transit point before our final trip to Germany. This new transaction in my life was something that caught me by surprise. I had not dreamed of going to Europe. I always desired to be close to my family and help get them out of poverty and suffering as I advanced in life.

Going to Germany with a friend who I had known for such a short time was another event that reminded me how unpredictable life can be. Sometimes we plan and set certain goals only to see another event get in the way. As a 15-year-old boy, I had no idea what was ahead of us in this trip. I had not traveled such a long distance and so was panicking.

According to Elisha, we were to travel by bus from Liberia to Niger, and this was going to take approximately two weeks if the buses were moving fast enough. We could not travel direct to Niamey, the capital of Niger; we had to pass through the nation of Ivory Coast (Côte d'Ivoire), which shares a border with Liberia. We were to pass through Ouagadougou, the capital city of Burkina Faso, and then finally arrive in Niger, where we would take a flight to Germany.

Hearing Elisha describe these different routes and the long distance we would have to cover by bus was frightening to me because I was inexperienced in traveling. I almost told Elisha that I wasn't going anymore. But looking at how much he had spent and sacrificed to help me, and considering the funds raised by my parents to help gave me a reason to stay positive and know that God was in control of the situation just as he had always been in control every other time. I had to stay positive, have faith, and trust God.

We had prayed and fasted and so there was a reason for God to watch over us—so Elisha would say. As I heard these encouraging words from him, my confidence and motivation began to grow again. I became even more confident as I thought of the opportunity Elisha mentioned about my dreams coming true and how I would be able to finish high school and go to Bible school.

Thinking of the high-quality education I would have in Germany and the ministry work I would be able to do gave me reason to quit all the worries, panic, and anxiety that I was having at that moment.

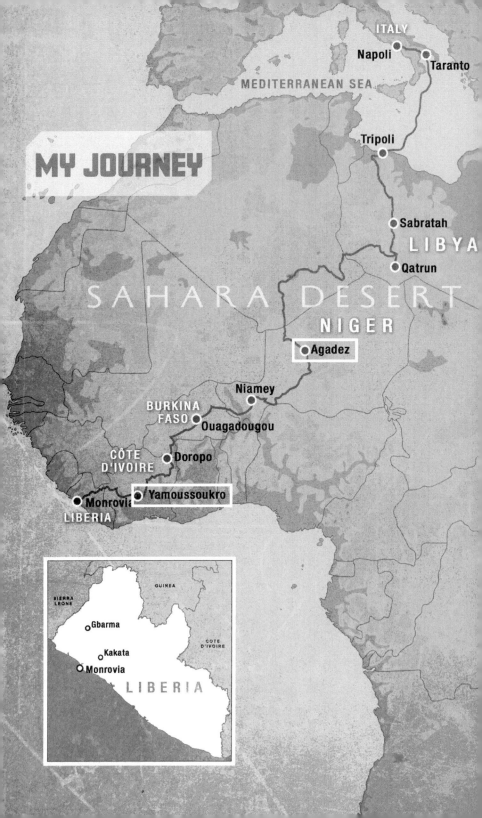

PERILS AMONG FALSE BRETHREN
CÔTE D'IVOIRE

My hope was strong. Our confidence grew, and the journey finally began. Our first travel plan was to pass through Yamoussoukro, the capital of Ivory Coast. From Monrovia, Liberia to Yamoussoukro is about 781 kilometers (485 miles) by bus, but it took us about four days due to the bad road systems we have in Liberia and the Ivory Coast.

IN PERILS OF ROBBERS

From Monrovia to the main border we share with Ivory Coast took us a day, and we had to sleep on our side of the border. After crossing the border, it took us another three days to get to Yamoussoukro. Our first experience in Ivory Coast didn't go as we expected. We were robbed, taken to the wrong destination, and made to spend an extra 248,850 CFA francs (equivalent to about $450).

All the nights we spent traveling through the Ivory Coast were rough ones. We were sleeping outside at the open bus stations because we had no money for hotels. Our luggage was not allowed to leave the bus because, according to the bus operators, we would be leaving early in the morning and they wouldn't have time to reload everyone's luggage. During this time, the only thing I could remember us doing was brushing our mouth, but for changing our clothes or taking a shower, that was impossible as all our things were in the trunk of the bus.

Going without changing or showering for nearly four days got me worrying again. The confidence I had was now going away. Knowing that we still had Burkina Faso to pass through, which I was told is hot with desert dust, as well as Niger, I began asking Pastor Elisha if this was how the rest of the trip was going to be. As he himself wasn't sure what lay ahead, he couldn't answer my questions. This again got me wondering if this trip was worth traveling.

What I noticed in this country was that most Ivorians were not friendly toward us. The bus operators and drivers were only after the money we had. We couldn't speak French, which is their official language, which made matters even worse for us. In all of this, the only thing I could think of was to pray because I knew if anything happened, only God could save us.

BUSES, BRIBERY, AND BEATINGS

After our four days in Ivory Coast, we took another bus to Burkina Faso. Our Burkina Faso experience was one I will never forget. As we sat in the bus all day, being so tired and hungry, all I could do was sleep even though it was very hot. Upon reaching the Doropo Kampti border, everyone had to come down from the bus for security purposes. And as we came down, everyone quietly walked in groups with their passports and bus tickets in their hands. Walking through the border, we were then held by the Burkina Faso police for reasons they refused to tell us. We had all the required legal documents plus our official country passports, but they still held us to question us.

After answering all their questions and giving legal proof of our traveling, they still would not let us continue. Being a French Muslim country and seeing that Elisha and I had our Bibles and were intending to preach the gospel, it became even more difficult for us. Not speaking French added to the complications and delay. They took our luggage and passports and put us in an isolated building.

The bus driver could not wait for us as the other passengers were already complaining, and he would not pay some of our money back either. There again we lost another good amount of money. We didn't have much money now and being only a short distance into the journey, Elisha became more concerned.

After spending the night in that isolated building and going all day and night without food, I was very tired with no energy to do anything. Looking at what we faced in the Ivory Coast and now in Burkina Faso, I became very discouraged and told Elisha we should tell the police that we wanted to go back to our country. But he insisted that this was just a minor issue and that God was in control.

The police came the next day, but they still did not give a reason for why they were holding us. After spending another half day in that place, we were given some water to gain energy and strength. As they came back to us, they requested that we give them $250 to be released. Elisha engaged them, saying that bribery was against our Christian faith and that he would appreciate it if they told us our crimes or anything illegal that we did. Seeing that we refused to give them the money, they began beating on us with their batons.

After beating and abusing us for about 45 minutes, they finally let us go with no explanation. As we were set free, we spent another day at the same border waiting for another bus so that we could continue our journey to Niger.

With the help of God, after a day, we were able to get a bus that had just one seat left. With no choice, I sat on Elisha's lap for the nearly four-hour drive. Being so tired and worried, I kept telling Elisha I wanted to go back to Liberia. This was too difficult for me as I had already experienced persecution back home and did not want to experience more. I was consumed with fear and uncertainty, and all my hopes and confidence were gone. Perhaps this was because of my inexperience in traveling, I don't know, but it felt horrifying considering the treatment we got in the first two countries we passed through.

I suspect that most of the bad treatment we received in these countries was because we did not speak French and were Christians with missionary intentions. These are Muslim countries that do not embrace the Christian faith and its practices. In all of this, we kept moving no matter how resentful they were toward us. As we continued our journey, we got another bus and headed to Ouagadougou, the capital of Burkina Faso.

In Ouagadougou, the police became suspicious upon inspecting my missionary certificate from James R. Davis Memorial Baptist Church and Elisha's pastoral ordination certificate. They held us for about three hours. After asking us a lot of questions pertaining to our travel and mission plan, they finally let us go without asking for money like the police at the border.

FROM BURKINA FASO TO NIAMEY, NIGER

At the border between Burkina Faso and Niger, we were again held for about six hours for questioning. We were about twelve days into our journey, and I was now very worried and extremely tired from the continued stress. I began telling myself that it was a mistake to leave Liberia and my family. I should never have agreed to come. Perhaps God has again turned his back on me and wants me to suffer and die in a foreign land.

As these thoughts went through my head, I lost my appetite. I couldn't eat because of the fear and worries that took hold of me. Elisha became worried about me and decided to call his brother. He had not called him since we started the journey because his brother told him he should only call once we got to Niger. This added to my panic because I doubted we were going to be able to reach his brother in Germany.

After our release at the Niger border, we got back on the bus and headed for Niamey, the capital of Niger. It was from this city that we were to take a flight to Germany. The reason for this long road travel to another country such as Niger from Liberia is because of the poor travel system we have in Liberia. To travel abroad from Liberia is nearly impossible if you do not know someone within the system. Thus, for we, the poor, to travel out to Europe, we must travel either to Ghana, Nigeria, or Niger to work out the visa process. I do not know how it all works, but I heard that is how it is often done. I believed this was the reason Elisha's brother wanted him to come this far in order to help get him to Germany.

Meanwhile, we arrived in Niamey, and Elisha tried
but was not able to reach his brother. Olsen did not
answer our calls for more than a week, leaving us to
suffer in a place where we knew no one. I couldn't
stand the stress anymore and ended up getting sick
with fever and headache. The little money we had
was nearly gone. The journey we thought would take
two weeks became a month and six days just from
Liberia to Niamey, Niger.

We had to stay in Niamey until I recovered because
there might be medical tests as part of the visa
process, according to Elisha. After a week, I
recovered, and we finally heard from Olsen, the
brother of Elisha. This time he told us that he would
like us to travel to a city called Agadez in Niger.

Agadez is a place full of Libyan and Nigerian rebels
and terrorists who oppose their governments.
It is known as a place without law and order.
Everyone does that which is right in their own eyes.
Considering this, I again grew fearful and told Elisha
going back to Liberia would be the best option,
that I didn't want to die. I had not heard from my

parents nor had they heard from us. Elisha had told them that we would only call them when we were in Germany, not knowing how long that was going to take. He was the oldest and my guide; my parents had entrusted me to him, and so I needed to obey every decision he made no matter the cost. I grew up under such rules, so it wasn't strange to accept difficult situations even if they did not favor me.

As I trusted Elisha, that's how he too trusted his brother. He had trusted everything his brother said and so advised that we should travel to Agadez as his brother wanted us to.

KIDNAPPED: FROM NIAMEY TO AGADEZ, NIGER

Not wanting to waste more time, we quickly found another bus and traveled for two more days through the hot desert to Agadez. There we were taken hostage by a group of men who claimed to be police. They took our luggage and passports, like at the Burkina Faso border. Unlike the Burkina Faso border police, however, the police here were very anti-Christian and corrupt. After taking our luggage and passports, they took us to a very isolated place they called their police depot.

Here we were beaten by five men with their batons and belts. Some of them spoke English, and their concern was that we came to pollute their country and region with the gospel of Christ. For this reason, they wouldn't let us go. They also claimed that our goal was to go to Libya and pollute with the gospel there as well. Hearing these words reminded me of Acts 17:6, and how Paul and Silas were accused of turning the world upside down with the gospel. It felt that God was right there, watching every scene along the way. We had now been persecuted based on our faith, not due to any form of illegal traveling activities.

They continued to insult and beat us with their batons, then went on to tear our Bibles apart, and after doing to us that which satisfied them, they began asking us if we had anyone in the area that we could contact. Elisha told them that his brother had given him a number to call when we reached Agadez.

Upon hearing this, they brought out our luggage, and Elisha was able to make the call. Within a half hour, a car came to pick us up. As the Lord lives, the man who arrived was the boss of the men who were beating us. His name was Abdou, a white Libyan who had lived in Niger for nearly all his life and had gained much power as one of the mafias in Agadez. We were taken to one of Abdou's many houses. This was the first time since leaving Liberia that I was able to take a good bath, eat, and sleep. The place was decent, but getting our visas to go to Germany was all we could think of. We had little money left, not enough to feed us and pay for our visa processing and plane tickets.

Elisha kept calling his brother to find out what our next steps were to get our plane tickets and visa. After four days, Olsen finally picked up the phone. His response was that all the money that we had left should be given to this mafia. I became afraid and so was Elisha. But he still trusted his brother and finally gave $1500 of the $2000 we had left to Abdou. As we soon discovered, Elisha's brother had been lying all the time about helping us get a flight to Germany.

Abdou received the money and I guess shared it with Olsen. We were later told that Abdou would take care of us by taking us somewhere that was not part of the agreement and discussion made back in Liberia. We had no idea of how this new person was going to treat us.

After another two days in Abdou's house, some nice-looking men in well-dressed suits came about 7 pm in the evening, claiming they had come to take us to the airport and that our tickets were ready. We got in a very expensive car like one I had never ridden in while in Liberia. We were given plane tickets that did look real but were actually fake. However, it all felt real and convincing at the time.

We drove for about an hour with no sign of an airport or sound of planes. I again became very afraid and so was Elisha. He held my hands and we prayed, asking the Lord to protect and save us from whatever we were about to face. After another 30 minutes, Elisha asked the driver where he was taking us. All the driver said was, "Be calm, you are in safe hands."

Elisha tried calling his brother again but couldn't
reach him anymore. We were now on our own, in
the hands of the Nigeran rebels. The promised trip
to Germany was all a lie. In fact, we were robbed
and sold into human trafficking by Olsen, Elisha's
cousin, whom he considered a brother.

IN PERILS IN THE WILDERNESS

"ONLY 1 IN 5 SURVIVE"

As we rode in the car for more than two hours, my level of panic and anxiety took over me and I started vomiting. I received my first slap in the face from them. When we reached a certain place, they took all the rest of the money we had, drew guns on us, tied our hands behind our backs, and put dark black bags over our heads. I was so scared and began crying. They tied my mouth so no one would hear and put us back in the car.

After another hour's drive, we arrived at a place with a lot of people. This was an isolated place in the desert, with no nearby towns or villages, and a four hours' drive from the nearest city. Some of the people were there against their will like us, and others willingly because they wanted to cross over to Europe from Libya, even though there was only a 20% chance of surviving the trip. We spent two days and nights here, sleeping on the ground without any cover and surviving on only water. We had no money left, and even if we did, there was no place to buy food.

"HOLD ONTO YOUR STICK"

After two days in this place without taking a bath or brushing our mouths, they came and put us on the back of a pickup truck. There were more than 40 persons squeezed together, each holding a two-liter bottle of water. They made us sit with our backs against each other, our legs outside the truck, and a stick between our legs to hold. That stick was said to be your means of survival. If you are not strong enough to hold onto it when the truck was moving, you will drop to the ground, and if you drop, the driver will not stop for you.

They tell you this in their Arabic language. People who understand Arabic will try to explain what is being said. Our interpreter said things like, "We are not a rescue team and so when you drop from the car, you will be left behind in the desert and will die, so hold onto your stick, only the strong survive." These words left everyone in fear. As we got on the truck, we had no idea how long this journey would take.

Experiencing these horrifying moments again soon after a few days of rest at Abdou's house reawakened my old memories of the many things I had experienced. I felt as one who was just created for the purpose of struggling and suffering through life. From birth to my 15 years of age, it seemed that all I had ever known was going through difficult times and situations that I could not control.

The few joyful moments I could recall were from times in my church, my community Bible studies and meetings, and with my parents for the first time after many years of not seeing them. The only place I ever found true comfort and inner peace was when I accepted the Lord Jesus as my Lord and personal Savior. He has been the reason behind every strength, energy, and every breath that I breathe along the way. His love, care, mercy, protection, and guidance has been the source of my strength and existence. His love and ways are far beyond men's understanding. We cannot fully comprehend His magnificent and infinite powers. As Psalm 139:6 declares, "Such knowledge is too wonderful for me; it is high, I cannot attain unto it."

When I consider my life, knowing where I came from, seeing how lost and dead I was in sin and how Christ saved me, it gives me more reason to love and trust and serve Him in every situation. Being kidnapped, traveling through the Sahara Desert, and sold into slavery, and yet being saved by God, is reason enough to serve and dedicate my entire life to Him.

The horrifying journey across the Sahara Desert took seven days. The sun burnt our bodies, and dust filled our eyes, nose, ears, and even mouth if you mistakenly opened it. During the day, the temperature ranged from 86 to 122 degrees Fahrenheit. At night, it dropped below freezing and could be very windy. It takes the grace of

God to survive here. Many do not make it to their destination alive. The human bones, skulls, and dead bodies that I saw lying in the desert was evidence of this. In fact, I saw two men shot because they would not comply with the driver. Their bodies were left behind in the desert too.

Killing is something most of these Arabs consider a way to please Allah, their God, helping them earn their way to heaven. This brought more fear to me because it was my first time to see such a sight. I remember Elisha trying to cover my eyes with his hands so I could not see what was going on, but one of the rebels beat his head with the edge of his firearm.

I became even more fearful. I thought, "If this happened to those men, it might happen to me." I was the youngest on the car, and very weak. Elisha was deeply worried about me falling to the ground and being left to die.

All I could think of was to hold onto my stick as instructed—and pray.

"IN DEATHS OFTEN"

This journey across the Sahara Desert was a time that I really saw God's protection in our lives, Elisha's and mine and the life of every other person who survived the desert and treatment we received from the rebels.

The harsh, difficult times I had experienced during our travels from Liberia to Niger could not compare to what I experienced in the Sahara Desert.

I had always doubted that miracles happened today even though my mom did believe in God's miracles and still does. I saw for myself that miracles do really happen. God is always there doing great things for us and on our behalf if only we trust Him with all our hearts, minds, bodies, souls, and spirits. He proved this to me during my desert experience.

All food and water were completely gone with two days still left to reach Libyan territory. I should not have survived this journey, but God saved and protected me from the hands of unkind and wicked men. Nearly dead, He revived me. With no one to turn to, He came to my rescue. Like Moses in the Bible, God took me from my Egypt and let me pass through my desert to prepare me for what lay ahead. We can always trust Him in everything no matter what the situation or circumstance is.

MY JOURNEY

ITALY
Napoli
Taranto

MEDITERRANEAN SEA

Tripoli

Sabratah

LIBYA

Qatrun

SAHARA DESERT

NIGER

Agadez

Niamey

BURKINA
FASO
Ouagadougou

CÔTE
D'IVOIRE   Doropo

Yamoussoukro

Monrovia
LIBERIA

SIERRA
LEONE   GUINEA

Gbarma

CÔTE
D'IVOIRE

Kakata
Monrovia

LIBERIA

IN PERILS BY THE HEATHEN

QATRUN, LIBYA

After seven days, we reached the border between Niger and Libya. Everyone's water was gone, and people were fainting and vomiting. I too vomited a lot. We continued the journey and we finally came to a place called Qatrun, a town in Sabratah state in Libya. In Qatrun, we were put into a small one-room building where we were left to spend the night. Then we were put into another vehicle and transported to the main city of Sabratah. In Sabratah, the rebels who brought us from Agadez turned us over to a black Libyan.

After Libyan president Muammar Gaddafi died in October of 2011, civil war broke out in the country. Each major city such as Sabratah now had their own leadership, and most of them were black or white Libyan rebels. Libya is known for its illegal human trafficking, buying and selling humans, as well as kidnapping people and then extorting money from them to obtain their freedom. Libya is also known for its persecution of Christians.

As we were given over to these new people, I had no idea we were again being sold. They spit on us and in our presence, burnt all our luggage and our Liberian passports. They also burnt our Bibles, which had been torn by the Agadez police. All my ministry documents, such as my Baptism certificate, missionary certificates, Sunday School and Children's Pastor certificates, our mission plans, and Pastor Elisha's Pastoral Ordination certificate were all burnt. Then Pastor Elisha and I were separated, and I was left alone. He had tried convincing the Arabs that I was his son and needed to be with him. But one of the men began to beat Elisha, shouting in Arabic, which we could not understand.

I cannot explain how horrible and terrifying it was to be separated from the one person that I had been looking up to for guidance. As I began to cry, these men started beating me with their big guns and spitting on me, and all the other men who were with us. I kept praying and crying for God's intervention as I was now alone with Elisha nowhere to be found.

We never saw each other again. It was a forever goodbye. I was now left alone among people I barely knew and with no way to contact my family in Liberia or Olsen, Elisha's brother.

After all our belongings were burned, I was left with only the seven days' dirty clothes I had from the desert journey. Alone and scared, I began calling on the Lord within my heart to deliver me from these wicked men who had no regard for others' lives. But as I prayed, hoping that God would intervene, the situation became even worse. They took me, along with the other men, and put us into a 40-foot container.

Sitting in that dark container, hungry and scared,
I could hear an engine and felt the container being
lifted in the air—I don't know if that was a Yellow
Machine or not. After the lifting came to a stop,
we sat in there for about an hour vomiting on each
other. Then they came and opened the container for
a few minutes to allow air to enter and then closed
it again. Then we began another journey that lasted
for roughly an hour.

Once we stopped, they opened the container and
put 25 of us outside. At this location, we were given
to another group of white and black Libyan boys
who were between about 20 to 25 years old. They all
had guns and were smoking as they took us and put
us into a pickup like the one we rode from Agadez to
Libya. In the pickup, they made us lie down flat on
our face over each other in the back of the pickup
and covered us with blankets so the Sabratah police
couldn't see us.

INTO THE LIONS' DEN

In all of these stressful moments, all I was thinking about was my family, how they might worry, having not heard from us. As we reached our final destination, we were told to come down quickly and run through a narrow gate to what looked like an unfinished building project. As we ran in the open gate, other Arabs inside quickly closed the gate after us.

The place did look like an unfinished house. It was full of Africans from many different countries. Some were kidnapped and sold into human trafficking like me. Others willingly paid money with the goal of going to Europe but were later tricked and kidnapped. I was the only Liberian among this group. The rest were mostly from Nigeria and Ghana, and some from other countries. Seeing this many people, I felt a little hopeful that I was now safe—but on the contrary, I was nowhere near being safe. In fact, I overheard my fellow prisoners say "Welcome to the lions' den."

The first welcome we received was a slap from each of the five Arab men who were in charge of this place. After slapping us, they told us to enter a long square room, where everyone slept. For two months I was in this place with no good food to eat. We were usually given a piece of bread to eat in the afternoon. We got drinking water from the bathroom from the same tap that supplied water for bathing and the toilet. Many got sick in there, and those who couldn't recover were taken to another location and left to die. They used to call this place "the room of no return." I saw more than three sick men taken to this room of no return, and they never came back.

At this moment, the only thing I could think of and pray for was for the Lord Himself to take my life. I prayed and prayed, yet my situation continued to get worse. During the two months I was held hostage, not a single day was I or any of the others allowed to go outside.

IN STRIPES ABOVE MEASURE

Our new captors demanded that we call our families and have them pay 3,000 Libyan Dinar (about 2,200 USD) into their account. Every morning, the Arab men who gave us the welcome beating would come with a roster and ask who had paid their money. If you tell them that you do not have a contact for your family or that they don't have the money to pay, they beat you on three places of your body—the first will be your back, the second will be under your feet, and the third will be your butt.

After a month, if you still haven't provided the money, they give you two options. One is to be sold to another person who is much more wicked and evil-hearted than they are. The second is to be put into a very dark underground hole that gets very hot during the day and very cold during the night. If you are placed in this hole, every day at least five men come to beat you and abuse you in any way pleasing to them. By the time they are done with you, your sense of knowing yourself will be nearly gone if you are not strong.

IN COLD AND NAKEDNESS

In my case, after a week and two days, I was asked to call my parents so they could send the 3,000 Libyan Dinar. I knew that fearing death or beating was not going to save me from these people. I told them that I did not have any way to contact my parents, which of course was true. I never owned a personal phone back in Liberia nor did my parents. I tried to explain this to a Nigerian who could speak both Arabic and English, and he told the boss, but this again created a much bigger problem for me. I was beaten severely until I bled from both my nose and mouth.

While bleeding, they sent me into the underground dark hole where people are put if they are unable to pay. Laying in this dark hold with no clothes, I began to slowly sing one of my favorite Christian songs, one that Mom used to sing for me at bedtime when I lived in the village. I knew going into this hole meant I would be beaten every day and might not survive. I was ready for death; I had already made up my mind with an open hand for death to take its course if it was the Lord's will. My heart was prepared, and my soul was ready to meet the Lord. Thanks be to God, I was already saved.

I kept reciting Corinthians 5:8 which says, "We are confident, I say, and willing rather to be absent from the body, and to be present with the Lord." This passage became the source of my strength as I kept reciting it. This is why I find it very important to memorize Bible verses because during your darkest hours, you can use them, and trust me, they can be very helpful in giving you confidence and boldness to face whatever you are going through.

After my first two nights in this dark hole, another man was brought in because he too had no money to pay. As we both spent the day in that pit, and after much weeping, I finally came to him and began to encourage him that God was in control. My voice could not come out well because of the hunger, thirst, and cold.

But as I slowly begin to share the word of God with brother Evans, a Nigerian, and encourage him, he started to have faith in God and began praying for God's peace. He was now confident that the Lord

Jesus was not leaving, just as he told the disciples in Matthew 28:20b "Lo, I am with you all the days—till the full end of the age." He was indeed with us. Evans and I spent about eight days in the dark hole before the Arabs started beating us and demanding that we call our family.

Our beatings continued for another week.

TRANSFERRED & TORTURED

After nearly a month in the hole, Abdullah, who bought me, took me out, made me shower, and then put me in the trunk of his car. After about 45 minutes' drive, he left me with another group of Arab men, and they took me to a place similar to the one we just left. The person I was sold to was Abdu Salam, a man who also owns a human hostage area most often called a connection house.

Because Abdu Salam had been told that I was unable to pay, he kept me in a very unhealthy building with no windows. They kept torturing me to call my family but realizing that I had no contact, Abdu decided to use me for any kind of work that he

had or someone had that might pay him money.
For three months, I worked for Abdu Salam taking
care of the poultry and doing various gardening
chores. He also had me work on his own farm
and sometimes took me to construction sites to
haul building bricks and cement. If he didn't have
someone with a job, he would take me to the labor
market and sell me for a week, after which time he
would come to pick me up.

Working for a Libyan, as a foreigner who has nothing,
they consider you a slave. You have to be very careful
and make no mistake because they will stone you or
beat you. If you ask them to pay you, they point their
gun at you. I did receive many slaps, beatings, and
stonings while working for Abdu Salam.

One night, I was very tired after working all day, and
the chain that Abdu Salam often put on my legs was
hurting me. I decided to call him to release it for me.
Hearing this request made him very upset, and he
nearly shot me with his gun. He pointed the gun at
my head and hit my head against the wall couple of
times and then ordered his boys to beat me. They

came right away and did to me as was instructed until they were satisfied. I began bleeding from my mouth and was filled with bruises all over my body. I could not sleep that night.

Early in the morning, Abdu Salam's boys came for me to go and work even though I had already worked for the money he wanted me to pay. That day, I could not work because of the pain in my body from the beating. When Abdu Salam learned that I wasn't able to work that day, he came and grabbed me by my shirt and spoke very angrily in Arabic. I knew this was not okay for me. All I could do was continue praying in my heart to the Lord. Abdu Salam put the chain back on my foot and locked me up again.

In the evening, his boys took me and put me in the trunk of their car. There was one who could speak a little English and he told me that Abdu Salam had instructed them to take me to his brother's place. His name was Muhammadu Salam.

OUT OF THE FRYING PAN?

During my first night at Muhammadu Salam's,
I heard that the Sabratah police were looking
for human trafficking places in order to free the
captives and send them back to their own countries.
I was very excited because this would mean seeing
my family again after seven months with no contact.
This excitement gave me so much confidence that
I began praying out loud. Before, I always prayed
silently, but this time, I had to voice it out. Five of
the people I met at Muhammadu Salam's connection
house were also Christians. As I was praying and
thanking God, they joined me.

When Muhammadu Salam's boys discovered that
we were praying in the name of Jesus, they became
very angry and started beating us. After beating us
with their guns, they asked who started the prayer.
Everyone was scared. They asked again, and I raised
my hand and said I was the one. My boldness made
them even angrier. They took me outside, removed
my shirt, tied my hands behind my back, put me
on the ground, and told me to stare at the sun as it

shines. Trying to refuse, they forced me to open my eyes to the sun, staring at the sun, and one of them asked me in their Arab tongue if I could "see Jesus." After mocking and spitting on me as they normally did, they took me back inside.

INTO THE FIRE

When Muhammadu Salam came, the boys told him that we had decided to do our Christian worship in the room with everyone. This made him angry, and he decided to take me to another location, another of his many human trafficking connection houses. As he was about to take only me, his boys told him that there were five of us. So we were all taken into the deepest part of the desert outside the city of Sabratah.

The Arabs here were the wickedest people I ever came across. In this place, I decided I will totally serve God no matter what situation I find myself in. I also decided I will give my entire ministry service to God by working with young people who need Christ and teaching them God's Word. Because when the devil takes over the lives and hearts of the youth, it becomes difficult to have a just and peaceful society.

After arriving at the new location, the first thing they did to us was shave our heads. We knew our persecution was about to start. After the shaving, they lined us up, removed our clothes, and rubbed some sort of stink-mud on us. Then they put us in a very small, isolated, dark room.

After few minutes, we started experiencing major discomfort all over our bodies. Our skin and heads felt as though they were on fire. The pain was very intense. Our eyes were closed, covered with the mud, and if we tried to open them, it felt like concrete cement was holding them shut. We were crying from the severe pain; our cries echoed all around. As we were crying and shouting, our captors laughed and mocked us about Jesus.

After nearly two hours, they brought us out, beat us, and used wastewater to wash the mud from our bodies. After this, they put us inside where the other groups were.

One day, I was called upon by one of the boys in charge of the area, a young teen like myself. He asked if I was the one that was praying at their boss Muhammadu Salam's connection house. I said yes, and he asked me why. I told him that because Jesus is my Savior, my God and Friend. I told him that Jesus had saved me at age 12 years old. He asked, "How did He save you?"

I began to tell him that He saved me by dying on the cross for my sins and the sins of the world, and after accepting and calling upon Him to come into my life to be my Savior, He became my Savior and Lord. He then asked me if Jesus was able to save me from them! My answer to him was that yes, Jesus was able to save me from them if He wills, but He can also choose to let them do whatever they want. This made him angry, and he slapped me and spit on me and called me a dog.

Later, they came to the room where we all were and asked us to call our family. As they came to me, I tried explaining to them my situation, that I had no way to contact my family. They said I was lying and gave me a good beating. After a while, one of them brought a phone so I could look for any of my friends or family members on Facebook. As I began to check, I could not find my big brother Junior. I told them none of my family members were on the Internet, but they insisted and kept beating on me.

After two days, they brought the phone to me again, and I started checking for some of my friends from my church in Liberia. While checking, I found my friend Michael Meyers who had once taken me off the street when I was homeless and gave me work and paid my school tuition as well. I quickly sent him a friend request from their phone, briefly explaining what had happened to me. After three days, Michael responded and agreed to go to my uncle's house.

RAISING THE RANSOM

Upon reaching them with the news, Michael was able to get my big brother Junior's phone number. Junior was now schooling in Monrovia. He quickly went to the village and told my mom and dad what had happened. Upon hearing the news, my mom suffered a heart attack and was taken to the nearby clinic. Dad called all his sisters and brothers for help raising the money. They were able to raise only $500 of the $2,200 my captors were demanding.

I told my captors what my family had raised, but they refused the $500 and insisted that I pay the full amount or they would kill me and throw my body in the desert. But I had already embraced death and so was no longer afraid of their threats to kill me. I could not do anything more because my family just did not have that much money. I just kept praying and quoting Scriptures to myself.

Muhammadu Salam normally came to this place only every three or four weeks. When he came this time, he agreed to take the $500 my parents had raised. The same day, my brother Junior sent the money to their account. Upon receiving the money, the boys decided behind Muhammadu Salam's back, since he had left again, to make me contact my family again for the rest of the money.

Since they refused to set me free, all I could do was to pray because I knew they might kill me at any time as they had others. I knew they were no longer holding me because I owed them money. It was something different, and I had to be prepared with my hope in Christ.

"ALLAH OR ISA—WHO DO YOU SERVE?"

A week after my payment, the boys in charge of the connection house called on me. They had discovered that I was praying again, and the others had joined me. Since we had violated their orders, we needed to be punished, and the punishment was death. I thought this was just one of their many mocking statements. However, they were serious.

They brought about ten of us outside and started questioning us to see how important we take our Christian faith. Each one of us answered in our own way because we knew death was involved. They then told us that before we are killed, we will suffer for eight days and on the ninth, we would be killed. We did not know how they were going to kill us. All we knew was that all of us were going to die within nine days.

Most of my friends were afraid, and some of them began to blame me because I brought praying in Jesus' name. But the five of us that Muhammadu Salam brought from the previous place were still confident and kept praying that the Lord Jesus' will be done.

The Arab boys told us that we would be killed because we were Christians, because we believed in Jesus Christ. Thus it was not for our praying, but rather for our faith in Christ, that we would die.

Mr. Victor, 35, years old; Daniel, 28 years; James, 30 years; Abeo 20 years; Isaac, 24; and me—we were ready for whatever we faced. It's not easy to be told you are going to be killed when you have committed no crime. Our lives were now determined by men who had no power to give one back.

After being told we would be killed in nine days, they stopped giving us our afternoon bread. For five days, they beat us under our feet, on our backs, and on our butts. On the sixth day, as they began persecuting us, the Arab boys began asking us,

"Allah or Isa Jesus—who is God? Who do you serve? Which is true—Christianity or Islam?"

The other five did not hesitate to deny Christ to save their lives. This was just the sixth day, we still had three more days, but they denied Christ.

We who kept strong were placed in another dark room. For the remaining two days, we were spit upon and became extremely hungry. Our mouths and throats were dry, and we had no energy. I personally felt as one who was already dead. My prayer was just, "Lord, let your will be done. Lord, please make me strong not to deny you. Lord, please take care of my family and take them from poverty. Lord, forgive my sins and accept me today! Thank you, Jesus."

Those were my prayers. Throughout my torture and abuse, I kept reciting Psalm 23. And also John 16:33 which reads, "These things I have spoken to you, that in Me ye may have peace, in the world ye shall have tribulation, but take courage—I have overcome the world." I was very scared and weak, but reciting these passages gave me courage to endure the pain and trial of testing that was awaiting me. Through the power of God, my friends and I kept our faith even though some are now with the Lord.

As we approached the ninth day, even though in pain, we kept praying and crying to the Lord for His will to be done. On the final day, they covered our heads and took us behind the building to where they had beheaded other Christians like us. They removed the bags from our heads and forced us to kneel down. As we kneeled down before the stool made for our beheading, they started mocking us and cheering and shooting their guns in the air and swinging their swords.

After making many jokes and mocking us and throwing the desert sand at us and spitting on us, they began asking us the same questions again: "Allah or Isa Jesus—Who is God and who do you serve? Christianity or Islam, which is true?" And we kept saying that we served Jesus and that we were Christians.

They asked who was the oldest among us, and Mr. Victor said right away that he was. They started by piercing him with the small knife they had.

At first our heads were bowed down, but as they begin killing Mr. Victor, they beat us to make us watch. It was a difficult sight to see as Mr. Victor was screaming for his life. At that moment, I felt very empty within myself.

As a 16-year-old boy, it was hard to watch someone's body parts being cut out by another human. I felt like my spirit had left my body and only emptiness remained. I was not myself anymore.

As they came to the next person, Brother James, I couldn't bear to see anymore. I quickly said that I was the one who started the prayer, but they refused to listen and went on to shoot James' two legs before skinning him alive from his neck to the chest. We were crying and screaming, and they were shooting their guns in the air.

As this is going on, Muhammadu Salam unexpectedly arrived. But it was too late, they had already killed Mr. Victor and James, and had shot one leg of Daniel.

When Muhammadu Salam saw what they had done, he was upset because it was not his order. They were supposed to free me right after my family had paid the $500. Muhammadu Salam angrily asked what the problem was, and they told him that we were being disobedient by not obeying their rules and that we were carrying on our Christian practices in the connection house.

After explaining to their boss, they took Victor's and James' bodies and threw them in the desert. Daniel was still alive and so was brought back to the connection house with us.

LEFT FOR DEAD

As the evening falls, something has happened. The boys' shooting drew the attention of the Sabratah police. Once Muhammadu Salam realized that the police were coming, they quickly put Daniel, Abeo, and me in their pickup to transport us to another location.

Daniel died in the car due to blood loss. After traveling more than an hour, I fainted from the stress of seeing and lying in Daniel's blood.

I eventually awoke from unconsciousness. Abeo and Daniel's body were lying next to me in a big trash dump. I believe they may have thought we all were dead.

Abeo and I slept.

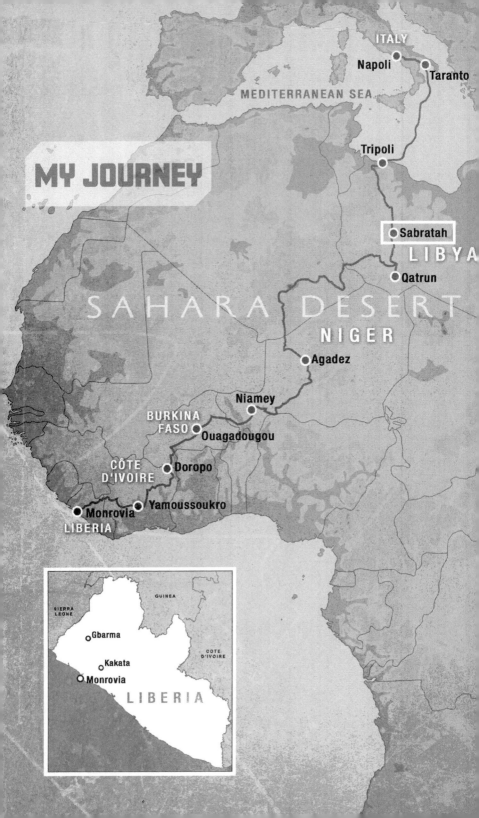

MY JOURNEY

ITALY

Napoli

Taranto

MEDITERRANEAN SEA

Tripoli

Sabratah

LIBYA

Qatrun

SAHARA DESERT

NIGER

Agadez

Niamey

BURKINA
FASO

Ouagadougou

CÔTE
D'IVOIRE

Doropo

Yamoussoukro

Monrovia

LIBERIA

SIERRA
LEONE

GUINEA

Gbarma

CÔTE
D'IVOIRE

Kakata

Monrovia

LIBERIA

IN PERILS IN THE CITY

SABRATAH, LIBYA

The next day, we were found by a Nigerian man whose name was Abaeze Adesina. According to Mr. Adesina, he was a little boy when his parents came to Libya. He had been living there for about 38 years. He took Abeo and me to his house and gave us water for bathing, fed us, and clothed us.

He had a car wash that he had been helping an Arab man manage. He asked us if we were willing to work there after we regained our strength. We said yes, we were willing to work and earn some money. After a week of recovery from all that we went through, he took us to the compound of the car wash where we began living and working.

The car wash had a room where all the washing materials were kept, and we were able to straighten the room and make it our new home. The next day, we were taught on how to wash cars and started working. Mr. Abaeze Adesina never told us how he planned on paying us or how the work system works. Due to his kindness toward us from the start and after spending a week at his place, we saw him as one we could trust.

After working for three months, we decided to ask him for our pay because we needed some money to buy some clothes. He had been giving us a little money to buy food, but had not given us our wages. When we asked him, he told us that we should ask the owner, Moha Hassan his boss, for our pay. But Moha Hassan was not the one who brought us here. In fact, we had no dealings with him. We were Mr. Adesina's workers; he hired us to work for him.

The truth is that Mr. Abaeze Adesina, who we thought was different from the Arabs, had been using us. He claimed it was to pay the expenses of the food and shelter he provided after finding us at the dump site. So our three months of hard labor, from 6 am to 8 pm, were to pay his own debts. We couldn't do anything but to make another agreement to work another three months for pay.

Working in car wash in Libya, especially in Sabratah where the rebels dominate, could be dangerous. Many times, the rebels would take advantage of us by having us wash their cars and then refusing to pay. If we asked them to pay, they would point their guns at us and tell us to get away. Sometimes, even if it was past time to wash cars in the night and the gates were locked, they came with their guns and insisted that we open the gate and wash their cars. This was a nearly daily experience, so Abeo and I were always prepared to wake up at any time of the night to wash cars for those rebels, sometimes for free. Mr. Adesina wasn't always at the car wash, so we had to deal with these threatening situations by ourselves.

One Saturday afternoon, at about 3:00, a fight broke out between Mr. Adesina and one of the rebels who refused to pay after we finished washing his car.

They exchanged gun fire, but pointed their guns in the air. Upon hearing the gun fire, the owner, Moha Hassan, came from his house across the street to calm things down. The rebel eventually left but came back the next day with reinforcements. About four cars came, full of heavy fire guns, and they began shooting at the gate at about 5 am while we were still sleeping.

Upon hearing the shooting, Abeo and I hurriedly ran outside and thank God, the gate had not yet fallen. We quickly found our way out the small gate at the back and ran to Moha Hassan's house to tell him what was going on since his house was closer than Mr. Adesina's. The rebels kept shooting at the gate, and we found the boss watching the rebels destroy his car wash from his house across the street. Afterwards, Moha Hassan blamed us for what had happened. When Mr. Adesina came, Moha Hassan told him to leave too because we all were responsible for the destruction of his car wash. This sacking of our boss Mr. Adesina led to another difficult time for me in Libya.

SOLD OUT AGAIN?

I had already seen how they treat foreigners and with the human trafficking being one of the leading businesses in Libya, you can easily be kidnapped and sold at any time. Being in the car wash was a bit safe for us because we were not being held hostage. But now we had no place to stay. Knowing our situation, Mr. Adesina decided to use the money we had earned to send my friend and me to Tripoli, to a friend he trusted, because Sabratah wasn't safe for us.

I was not convinced his words were true because he had already tricked us once by making us work for three months without pay, which ended by him making us work another three months. I personally couldn't agree with Mr. Adesina's proposal—I had already experienced a lot of difficult times due to trusting people. I once trusted my uncle and he let me down causing me to become homeless. I trusted Elisha who trusted his brother, and at the end, I went through much persecution and suffering. So trusting Mr. Adesina's words was something I found quite difficult.

Meanwhile, Mr. Adesina had our three-month's pay.
He refused to give it to us. He said that the only
thing he could do for Abeo and me was to send us to
Tripoli where his friend lived, the one he said would
help us. Since we could do nothing else, we agreed
to his plan.

After spending two days at his house, Mr. Adesina
put Abeo and me in the trunk of his car, which we
knew was not a good sign. Being locked in the trunk
of a car in Libya implies one of two things: Either
you have been kidnapped and are being transported
to be sold or you have already been sold to a person
and are being transported to another connection
house. Abeo and I were convinced that we were
being sold again but this time, by our own African
brother.

Going through this moment again, I began praying
and asking God not to allow my friend and me to
experience again what we had experienced before at
the hands of human traffickers. From October 2015,
when Elisha and I left Liberia, until now, April 2016, I
had been suffering. This time I began praying to God

to send me back to Liberia with no idea how that was going to happen.

IN HUNGER AND THIRST

Mr. Adesina drove Abeo and me to another connection house and left us there with a Ghanaian man named Eric Oluoch. He owned this place and was responsible for transporting people who are either sold into human trafficking or are trying to cross over to Europe by sea from Libya. That same night, Abeo and I were put in another car with other Africans to be transported to Tripoli.

Mr. Adesina had purchased food for us to take along. However, the Arab men who were taking us to Tripoli took our food, ate some, and threw the rest on the road.

I nearly fainted in the back of the car they put us in. Hungry, tired, and weak, I could do nothing. I began screaming because there was no air to breathe. We were many, and the space was very small. We were on top of each other, and they told us not to talk. But I was suffocating and began shouting, which led to me nearly being killed by the Arabs who were transporting us. They stopped the car and came back, angrily asking who was screaming. The other men all pointed to me, and this led to an intense beating.

After beating me, they closed the car trunk and we began going again. After we passed a police checkpoint, they would open the trunk to let air in and then closed it again.

This time, we drove for about three hours without them opening the trunk. We began vomiting from lack of air. After a long night of travel, we finally got to Tripoli, and everybody was separated and given to different drivers including my friend Abeo.

This was another painful moment. During our seven months in Sabratah, from the persecution at the connection house to the car wash, Abeo and I had done everything together, including praying, cooking, and eating from the same bowl. It felt as though we were blood brothers, and so separating us, especially not knowing where we were going, was painful. We shed tears and begged the drivers

to send us to the same location, but they responded
with slaps to our faces and ears.

SLAVERY AND ESCAPE

Abeo was now gone, and like when Pastor Elisha
and I were separated, I was again alone and lonely.
I was finally brought to a place called Sharia as-
Sayidi, Tarabulus, in Tripoli to an Arab man named
Mohammed Ahmed. This man had a welding shop
and needed someone to work for him.

When he discovered that I was new to welding, he
wanted to sell me to someone else to get back the
money he had paid to purchase me from my former
boss Mr. Adesina in Sabratah. But his son, who was
taking care of the shop, said that I should stay. So
far, he was the only good Arab person that I came
across during my time spent in Libya. Al-Ashab
Ahmed was his name. He and I worked together, and
he taught me how to do welding.

However, his father was not always satisfied with
me just doing one job. He wanted to use me to get
his money back. I was his slave, thus he would send

me to his family's water company to work there
and then take whatever money I made. But his son,
Al-Ashab, developed a love and care for me and was
against his dad's harsh treatment of me.

After spending one month and two weeks constantly
working, Al-Ashab decided to take me away from his
cruel father. When he told me this, I did not know
what his plan was. He only told me that I should
be ready any time, that he was going to help me
escape. I asked, "Escape to where?" because I had
nowhere to go nor did I know anyone in Tripoli other
than his family.

After a few days, at about midnight, he came to
the shop where I used to sleep and woke me up
to escape with him. I quickly got up not knowing
where he was taking me. I was very afraid because
if his father caught us, he would probably kill me for
trying to escape.

As I followed Al-Ashab Ahmed that night with friends
he brought, they took me to an unfinished building
to stay until those who were supposed to pick me up

came. They left, and I ended up spending the night there alone.

This was one of the moments again that I experienced the protective hand of God over my life because Libya, especially Tripoli, can be very dangerous at night.

Nobody is to be out after 8:00 p.m. because of the Tripolitan rebels. That's when most of the kidnapping and killing go on, during the dark hours.

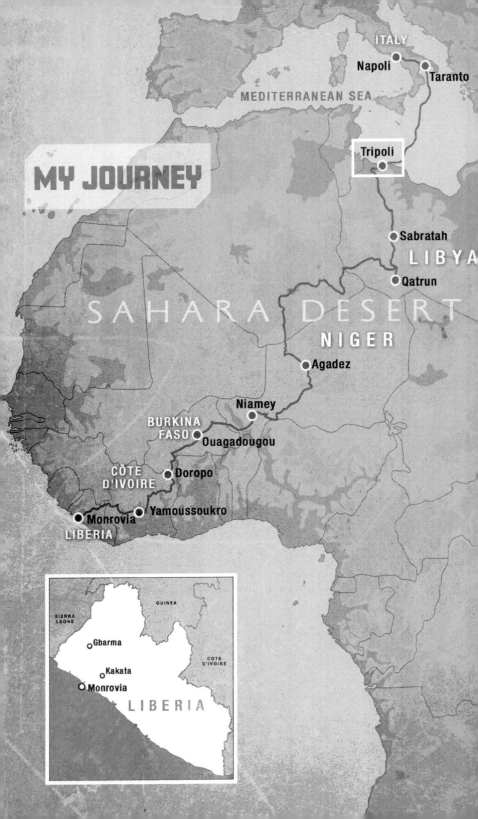

IN PERILS
IN THE SEA

TRIPOLI TO TARANTO

Early the next morning, three men came and told
me that Al-Ashab Ahmed had told them to take
me to the seaport for most of the illegal crossings
to Europe. Since many Africans travel from their
countries through the Sahara Desert to Tripoli for
the purpose of crossing over to Europe, Al-Ashab
Ahmed thought I was one of those and that my
reason for being in Tripoli was to cross illegally to
Europe.

As I heard this, it got me more afraid because I had
heard that crossing the sea with the flimsy rubber
dinghy boats they use meant only a 20% chance
of survival. I told them that I wanted to go back to
the shop, and they told me yes, we will take you to

the shop if that's where you want to go. But it was all lies. After sitting in the car, they drove past the shop and never stopped. I was again very scared not knowing what they were going to do with me.

After traveling for about three hours, they took me to a site where I met hundreds of Africans from different countries whose goal was to cross over to Europe by boat. I spent about a week there with no food or money to buy any. I had to beg some of the people I met there to give me some of their food or leftovers if any. Staying here was like the times in Sabratah. We would be in the sun all day, with temperatures up to 115 Fahrenheit, and in the night, it got very cold. With no blanket to cover me, I spent most nights sitting near the cooking fire to try to stay warm.

After a week, the men took me to the seaport where I also met a lot of people. At the seaside, they put me in a group of men, some old and some young like me. Given that I was among these people, I felt safer. Later I was taken with 15 other men to the main crossing spot where they turned us over to an

Arab man named Aaftab. He was the one said to be in charge and responsible for illegally transporting people over to Europe by a flimsy rubber dinghy, or one might call it an inner tube boat.

The night, which was Saturday June 25, 2016, was another time of my life that I had nothing more to do but trust God to save me. I had not been on the sea. I had only swum in rivers and that was when I was little, back in the village.

The huge Mediterranean Sea was a scary sight to behold, and I became very frightened. Using a flimsy rubber dinghy to cross the Mediterranean Sea is very risky. When they put you in the dinghy, the Arabs remind you that your chance of survival is only 20% so if you are not careful, you will die on the sea. Also, they say things like "Be careful not to be caught by the Libyan police because if caught, you will be brought back and put into prison or even killed." Hearing these warnings from the Arabs themselves made me even more frightened about the crossing.

A MIGRANT RAFT & RESCUE SHIP

(Shutterstock)

(Shutterstock)

I had been advised by one of the men I met at the sea to not by any means talk about being taken back to Tripoli, no matter how frightened I was, because saying this will mean my death. They don't take you back once you are brought to the seaside for crossing. According to him, either you agree to cross or they shoot you in the head.

This was indeed true. That night, with my own eyes, I saw a young man shot in the head because he was too afraid to get on the flimsy rubber dinghy boat. Beholding such a horrifying sight, I could do nothing more than comply with whatever I was told to do.

The reason they won't take anyone back is because the business they are doing is illegal and having migrants in their cars going back to Tripoli means paying extra money to the Libyan police or hiding them like they did with us when coming from Tripoli.

I had to deal with the situation by accepting what was before me at that very hour and moment.

"I WILL MEDITATE ALSO OF ALL THY WORK, AND TALK OF THY DOINGS"

All I thought about at this moment was my family I left back home in Liberia, my church and friends as well as Elisha. Many thoughts kept running through my mind. I thought about all the dreams and goals I had in Liberia of preaching the gospel and helping my family to take them from poverty.

I also began thinking about how the Lord had protected and saved me on many occasions such as from my uncle's wife, being taken from the street as a homeless boy, saving Elisha and me from the Ivory Coast through Burkina Faso, Niger and the Sahara Desert, many persecutions in Sabratah, nearly suffocating in a car many times as well as from my boss Ahmed in Tripoli.

Reflecting on everything the Lord had delivered me from gave me the courage to face my fears that night and know that God was in control of my life. He had promised He would not leave me nor forsake me if I trust in Him. Thus, I needed to play my part by trusting in Him.

A NIGHT AND A DAY IN THE DEEP

As the time came for us to be put on the flimsy rubber dinghy boat, they brought about a hundred of us out with two Gambian boys who knew nothing about sailing a boat and another with a compass for direction.

As we were brought out, they immediately instructed us to get on the raft. After climbing in the boat it started leaking and they had to change it and give us a new one.

After all of the people piled into the new raft, at about 10 pm, we embarked on one of the riskiest journeys I have ever had in my life. After we sojourned for about 45 minutes, we could no longer see any light except for the moon that was shining that night.

We were all now alone, with everyone praying to their God. The Muslims began praying and calling on Allah while we Christians began praying and calling on the Lord Jesus to save us.

After three hours, many became seasick and began vomiting. After another four hours, the boys rowing the boat became tired, and a Nigerian man took over.

Later a fight broke out and one of the ladies on the boat fell into the water. The men on the raft quickly grabbed her hands and pulled her back into the boat, but during this time, the compass dropped in the water, our only means of direction.

I stood up in the boat the entire night, meditating on and reciting Bible verses for God's protection.

About 6 am, our boat began leaking air. The sea water started coming into the boat, and both women and men began crying and screaming for help.

In the process of this, we noticed a ship but were not sure if it was a rescue ship from Europe or if it was a Libyan ship. We all became afraid and stopped screaming.

(Back in Libya at the crossing point, we were advised
to not call out for help if we see a ship until we are
sure it is a European rescue ship.)

For this reason, we all kept quiet even though a lot
of water was coming into our boat. It would have
been better to die in the water than be rescued by
the Libyan Coast Guard.

(That would mean a constant suffering and pain at
the hands of the Libyan soldiers as they often abuse
women and children.)

We saw the ship come towards us, which led to
more fear and panic. One of the guys jumped
into the water to avoid being taken by the Libyan
soldiers.

However, it wasn't a Libyan Coast Guard rescue
ship. It was a Spanish rescue ship. As they
approached us, they spoke in both English and
French asking if we could understand.

Upon hearing them tell us to stay calm and that
they have come to rescue us, we all began to shout

with joy and a heart of thanks to God in our own languages and tongues.

We were transported by smaller boats onto the Spanish ship and given some medications and medical tests. Many had already fainted. I got sick and was taken into the emergency room of the ship. They gave me some medication and an injection that made me sleep.

I slept for about two hours and was then given food to eat, but all the stress caused me to lose any appetite for food.

We were on the Spanish ship for three days.

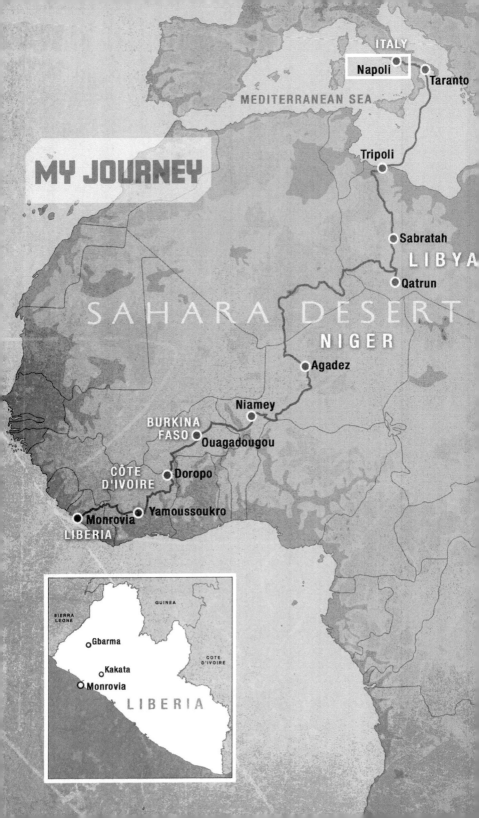

MY JOURNEY

ITALY
Napoli
Taranto

MEDITERRANEAN SEA

Tripoli

Sabratah

LIBYA

Qatrun

SAHARA DESERT

NIGER

Agadez

Niamey

BURKINA
FASO
Ouagadougou

CÔTE
D'IVOIRE
Doropo

Yamoussoukro

Monrovia
LIBERIA

SIERRA
LEONE

GUINEA

Gbarma

CÔTE
D'IVOIRE

Kakata
Monrovia

LIBERIA

THE CARE OF ALL THE CHURCHES

TARANTO TO NAPOLI

On the 28th of June 2016 we finally landed in Taranto (Italy) and were turned over to the Italian government. As we came off the ship, we were taken to different emergency camps. Teens and underage youth were taken to one place, while the adults were taken to another. Once we entered the emergency camp, they registered us and gave us clothes, a toothbrush, soap, and shampoo for our shower, and assigned us to a bed inside a tent.

During my first night in the camp, I could not sleep due to nightmares. The moment I closed my eyes, I kept seeing and re-living all the persecution and harsh treatment I had received all along the way from Liberia. The people in charge had to come and take me from the tent because I was frightening and disturbing the others.

For an entire week, this kept happening and many thought I was going mad. I was taken to a separate place to sleep at night, and security personnel would guard the door. They kept me in total isolation as I didn't want anyone around me. I felt very scared and insecure even though I was now safe, out of Libya. I was constantly checked by the emergency doctors. While panicking and being afraid, the only thing that helped me stay calm was reciting Isaiah 41:10 which says,

> Fear thou not; for I am with thee: be not
> dismayed; for I am thy God: I will strengthen
> thee; yea, I will help thee; yea, I will uphold thee
> with the right hand of my righteousness.

This verse was one of my sources of strength as it helped me focus and not panic.

After another week in the camp, on a Sunday evening, a missionary came to minister the Word of God to us, and this was the most beautiful and exciting moments I had had in a long time. That day

was very special to me because I was again able to
sit and listen to someone preach the Word of God to
me—the first time in nearly a year.

After the message was delivered that Sunday
evening, I went to the preachers right away and
asked if they could give me a Bible. I had been
without a copy of the Scriptures since my Bible was
burnt in Sabratah, when Elisha and I were separated.

Seeing my interest in God's Word, the preacher gave
me a Bible. I began reading it immediately, even
though the nightmares were still troubling me. On
the next Sunday, the same missionaries came again
to the camp. This time, I was given the privilege to
do an opening prayer and the Scripture reading. This
gave me courage to start ministering to people in
the camp.

After another week, I asked the camp director for
permission to start an evening Bible study and
prayer meeting like I did back in Liberia when I was
14 years old. As we began the Bible study, many of
the Christians who were there began to attend and
the number grew.

"WHO IS WEAK, AND I AM NOT WEAK?"

One evening, after I had taken a shower, I collapsed; I couldn't walk or move. I was taken to the Taranto Santissima Annunziata Hospital where I spent nearly a month. According to the doctor, my body was experiencing intense pain due to the intensive stress I had undergone. After I was discharged, I was transferred to a real refugee camp, where I spent another year and six months.

This camp was in Massafra, a small town in the province of Taranto of the region of Puglia, Italy. I was now able to attend church. However, all the churches around me were Catholic, since Italy is, of course, a Catholic country. I visited several, but just could not find my place. They all felt like my uncle's Catholic church, where the full counsel of God's Word was not being taught. So instead, I started a Bible study and Sunday evening worship service in the camp, as well as prayer meetings via local phone calls.

After eighteen months in the Massafra camp, I was able to obtain my Italian permit of stay, known as the Permesso di Soggiorno. My main goal of leaving Liberia to travel to Germany with Pastor Elisha was to get a quality education and be trained to become a good teacher of God's Word and preacher of the gospel of Christ Jesus. I decided it was time to leave the camp because there was no church or ministry that I could serve in. Since I had been in a Baptist church in Liberia, I began checking for Baptist churches in Italy.

GOD'S PROVISION IN NAPOLI

As I began to check for a Bible-teaching and preaching church, I got in touch with an online ministry that connected me with Bible Baptist Church in Napoli (Naples). I immediately checked their web page and found their contact information. With no time wasting, I decided to call.

After two days, I finally got a response from the pastor of the church, Pastor Matthew Olsen. We chatted several times over about two weeks, and then he invited me to pay a visit to the church. On February 8, 2018 I decided to visit. My trip went great. I was able to meet with the pastor and after much conversation, we agreed that I should come back in early March, after I had sorted out all document issues with the camp.

In March of 2018, I was finally able to move over to Napoli. I was now 18 years old. I had no money to rent my own house, so I was taken in by a brother from the church named Michael. After spending a week with Michael, I moved in with another generous brother named Isaac. While in Brother Isaac's house, I began looking for a job so I could find my own place to stay. Unfortunately, I couldn't find a job due to the difficulty of finding work in the area.

In Napoli, and Italy as a whole, finding a job as a black African immigrant is not easy. I began to worry because I had no idea where I was going to stay to continue at Bible Baptist Church. This new church I joined was a small church that really was not able to help me. But as the Lord lives, I came across a very loving, caring, kind, and generous person who through the Lord's grace saw a need of me being helped. We started talking and within a very short period, she became more than a great help to me.

She became a mother, a true friend, and a supporter who only saw the best in me and wanted to help bring my dreams to pass. Ms. Jane Albright, who came to work for the U.S Navy in Italy and attended Bible Baptist Church where I am a member, is someone whom I will never forget in this life or the next to come. Ms. Jane has been the reason for some of my dreams coming true.

Ms. Jane willingly took me into her house, fed me, and clothed me. She also helped me to complete my high school education through the online, American "The Keystone National High School," and I received my high school diploma in September 2019. She also helped me apply and get accepted into the renowned Moody Bible Institute in Chicago.

However, I was unable to attend Moody because the U.S consulate here in Napoli denied me a student visa. This was another time when I felt my dream of going to a Bible school was being shattered. But I could do nothing about it. I had to be courageous and have faith like every other time and know that God is in control and has a bigger plan for me than I can imagine.

NEW HOPES AND NEXT STEPS

I have been in Italy for about four years now, serving the Lord at Bible Baptist Church (BBC) in multiple areas, as the music and sound system operator/director, Sunday school teacher, and preacher on Sunday mornings, when given the opportunity.

Although my dream of going to Moody Bible Institute was denied, I have been able to take a three-year, college-level Bible certificate program from Faith Bible Institute through my church. I graduated in December 2020, having studied the Bible in depth from Genesis through Revelation. I have seen God work in wonderful and mysterious ways during my life and ministry here in Italy.

However, I still find one very important thing missing pertaining to my dreams, and that is ministering to teens and youth. BBC is a very small church with no youth department or ministry. This

dream for ministry is very important to me and I do
think and pray to the Lord every day about it.

Because of what I have seen back in Liberia and
Libya, I have come to understand that one of the
major reasons that our society is filled with evil and
unspeakably shameful things is because today's
young generation has drifted from the truth that is
in the Lord Jesus and His Word, the Bible.

Stealing, robbing, creating chaos, and making
communities unsafe to walk in during the evening
and early morning hours are mostly due to young
people whose hearts had been overtaken by evil
and the lies of the devil. Much of the persecution
I experienced in Libya was from young people like
myself. As I saw what these young people were
doing to me and to others within their own country,
I wondered why they were that way.

As I pondered this question, the answer I got again
and again was that they lack the fear and knowledge
of God and the love of Christ. This leads many to
destroy themselves and others.

Today around the world we find that most dark, ungodly, hateful, and wicked acts are done by young people. This is because our present generation of young people has been deceived by the devil and because many hearts have been taken over by the evil of this world. Without the fear of God, many destroy themselves.

If the people come to Christ when they are young, they will experience a change of heart and desire to live according to God's moral standards, and life will be better for everyone.

As I behold these things and know how they have affected our society, I have purposed in my heart that my main ministry work in the future, Lord willing, will be with youth, winning as many as I can to the Lord Jesus Christ.

LET NO MAN DESPISE THY YOUTH

That is why at age 14, I started a community Bible study for youth in my home country of Liberia, which led many to give their lives to Christ.

That is why also when I was in the emergency camp in Taranto, I began teaching the Bible to the few young people that were there.

That is also why, when I was brought to Massafra camp, I started both an in-camp Bible study with the few youth that were there as well as those I was able to contact via an online local conference call meeting.

That is also why I try to stay in touch with as many young men and women or boys and girls like me, to tell them of the amazing gospel of our Lord Jesus Christ and help them grow in their faith.

All this is not by my might nor by my power, but by the spirit and power of the Lord Jesus, Who has put this hunger in me to do His will and work here on earth.

It is my burning desire to work with young people from every walk of life to teach and tell them about Jesus. My prayer is that the Lord Jesus will direct my steps according to His will and lead me to the exact place He wants me to work with the potential and grace He has given me.

I pray and hope He will help me find that ministry where I can be able to serve and work with my fellow young people and make this dream a reality through the power of the Lord Jesus Christ.

With all of this, I still see the Lord working in my life as He makes a way out of no way time and time again.

"THE CONCLUSION OF THE WHOLE MATTER: FEAR GOD, AND KEEP HIS COMMANDMENTS"

Life is short but with God in it, it becomes more than amazing to live. The world without Christ leads to evil and chaos, a heart without Christ, the fear of God and the knowledge of his Word becomes evil and ends up destroying itself.

That's why every person, every family, every home, every community, and every nation needs Christ. We can do nothing without Him.

For the two decades I have lived on this earth, one important truth I have learned is that all lives need God and our souls need His saving power through His Son Jesus Christ.

My prayer is that we all will come to a realization that there is something more important than anything in this world—and that is accepting the Lord Jesus Christ and being saved by His precious blood.

SPECIAL THANKS
& ACKNOWLEDGMENTS

The Lord has wonderfully blessed me by bringing into my life Ms. Jane Albright and through her, a very generous church family in Christ, Calvary Church of Port Orchard in Washington State, which has been selflessly supporting me both financially and with prayer.

I am also grateful to be connected with their pastor, Pastor Kevin Lea, who has become an amazing spiritual mentor, educator, and advisor to me.

Thank you so much also to Ms. Rosemary McNonagle, who has generously supported me in amazing ways.

Thank you to my dear friend and supporter, Ms. Lynn Whiteaker from BBC. Ms. Lynn has been a great support to me since we became friends and has helped me experience the fellowship we have as one family in Christ.

I also want to thank Pastor Matthew S. Olsen and his wife Diane for their encouragement and help and by teaching of the Word of God to me.

Thank you also to my dear friend and sister-in-Christ, Amanda Pereira Schmoyer and her husband, Mr. Ian Schmoyer. Thanks so much for your prayers, counsel, and support.

May the Lord bless you all.

AFTERWORD

PASTOR KEVIN LEA

I met Abraham through Jane Albright (whom Abraham calls "Mom"), who had been a faithful congregant in our church for several years before job transfers took her to the Midwest and then to Italy. Because of our past pastor/congregant relationship, Jane first emailed me about Abraham in April of 2018, telling me how impressed she was with this young man. Then on May 1, she called with Abraham on the line to let me talk to him.

After that first conversation, I told Jane that I was willing to disciple Abraham if he were interested; I knew that my time with him would not be wasted. Abraham was eager to accept because he had many questions that he had about spiritual matters and the Bible.

During our subsequent discipleship sessions by phone and email over the next months and years, I became even more impressed as I saw the powerful hand of God upon him. In my nearly three decades of being a pastor, I had never seen this kind of godly character and profound hunger to learn God's word. He was driven to know the Lord Jesus in a deeper way and to know how to accurately share the gospel with others, even though he was only a teenager.

Early on, I asked him about the circumstances that brought him to Italy. His spoken English skills were not as they are today, and I had a difficult time understanding him over the phone. What I could gather was that he had joined with a pastor friend and fellow Liberian to go to Europe so he could further his Bible studies. However, he ended up enslaved by Libyan rebels, eventually escaping to Italy on an inflatable raft. I encouraged him to write out his story because I wanted to know the details of what happened, but he put it off, wanting to talk about his Bible questions instead.

In late 2019, Jane came to Washington on vacation to visit her son. A health emergency, surgery and chemotherapy resulted in her never returning to Italy. For the next few months, Abraham watched over Jane's apartment and oversaw the movers coming to box up "Mom's" stuff to ship back to America. Not a single item was missing when Jane received her things from the movers, and she was refunded the entire amount of her house rental security deposit. I was not surprised at this demonstration of integrity.

With Jane now back working in Washington and attending our church again, she approached our church leadership with the idea of applying for Abraham to come to our church as an apprentice Christian minister on an R-1 visa. We were excited to support this effort.

In early July, 2020, Jane again encouraged Abraham to write out his autobiography so that we could include it with the application. This time, Abraham complied and sat down to write this account, which we now know must have been a very difficult and emotionally traumatic reliving of the torture and horrors he experienced.

I had known Abraham for more than two years and had many conversations and emails with him. He was full of the joy of the Lord. He was thoughtful of others, prayerful, humble, never exhibiting bitterness or hatred, wise way beyond his years, never complained, and never played the victim, even though we now know that he had been a "victim" from the day he was born.

It is my prayer that this book will minister to all who have suffered the pains of this life and have been unable to heal from their effects. Jesus suffered even more than Abraham, as He took our sins upon Himself so that all who repent and put their trust in Him can be saved from sin and death. 1 John 4:19 says that we love Him because He first loved us. When we put our faith in Him to save us from our sins, Jesus sends the Holy Spirit to change and begin healing our hearts. He will replace bitterness with love—and self-centeredness with compassion for others—just as He has in Abraham's life.

Have you repented of your rebellion against God? Do you trust in the resurrected Jesus to forgive you and give you everlasting life? If not, why not? There is only one Physician who can change a heart of sin into a heart of love. None of us know how long we have left to live on this earth. Please humble yourself and receive His saving and healing power before it is too late.

> *"Now then, we are ambassadors for Christ, as though God were pleading through us: we implore you on Christ's behalf, be reconciled to God. For He made Him [Jesus] who knew no sin to be sin for us, that we might become the righteousness of God in Him."*
>
> —2 COR 5:20-21 (NKJV)

Pastor Kevin Lea

Calvary Church of Port Orchard, Washington

July 2021

QUESTIONS
FOR REFLECTION & DISCUSSION

1. Does Abraham's testimony change how you feel and respond to difficulties and hurts in your own life? Discuss or write out your thoughts.

2. Why do bad things happen to good people? Is God to blame? (Why or why not?)

3. How should Christians respond to evil and wickedness in this world? Is there any earthly hope? What is the ultimate solution?

4. How can the body of Christ be better equipped and prepared for ministry in these increasingly perilous times?

5. What do you feel led to pray for and do as a result of reading Gabriel's testimony?

6. What are some Scriptures you would like to commit to memory so that you will always have God's Word hidden in your heart?

To find out what the Bible says about these questions and share your own thoughts and questions, go to SoldOutServant.net.

GOD'S PROMISES TO FAITHFUL FOLLOWERS OF JESUS

"If the world hates you, you know that it hated Me before it hated you. If you were of the world, the world would love its own. Yet because you are not of the world, but I chose you out of the world, therefore the world hates you. Remember the word that I said to you, 'A servant is not greater than his master.' If they persecuted Me, they will also persecute you. If they kept My word, they will keep yours also."

—John 15:18-20a

"Beloved, do not think it strange concerning the fiery trial which is to try you, as though some strange thing happened to you; but rejoice to the extent that you partake of Christ's sufferings, that when His glory is revealed, you may also be glad with exceeding joy. If you are reproached for the name of Christ, blessed are you, for the Spirit of glory and of God rests upon you. On their part He is blasphemed, but on your part He is glorified."

—1 Peter 4:12-14

WANT TO BE "SOLD OUT?"
JOIN THE NETWORK!

To receive updates on Gabriel's journey, watch videos from the author, download resources, or order copies of this book, please visit:

WWW.SOLDOUTSERVANT.NET

ABOUT THE AUTHOR

Born in Monrovia, the capital city of Liberia in West Africa, Gabriel Abraham Singbeh did not talk or walk for several years. Considered cursed at birth by his tribe, his family was shunned and forced out of their community. Suffering separation from his parents at an early age, he was nine before seeing anything powered by electricity.

Gabriel was loved by his mother who always spoke of God, but he was abused by extended family with whom he lived. At age 15 he and a mentor, Pastor Elisha, set off for Europe in search of work and a Bible education, but along the way, were tricked by Elisha's cousin and sold into slavery. Repeatedly robbed, starved, tortured and trafficked through the Sahara Desert, Gabriel continuously called on God for deliverance.

After suffering for many months at the hands of merciless Muslim captors, enduring the terror and trauma of their inhumane acts, Gabriel was finally rescued, along with other refugees, from a sinking raft in the Mediterranean Sea. After partially recovering at an emergency camp, he eventually found comfort at a church in Italy, where an American believer befriended him as a second mother. Throughout his trials, Gabriel's hope and prayer has always been to serve God in youth ministry.

Now 21 years old and so far denied permanent asylum in Italy, (where it is nearly impossible for immigrants to find work), Gabriel faces great hardship and possible deportation. He is currently waiting for the Lord to open a door for him to receive further ministry training and experience. For details on how you can pray for and support his continuing journey, visit *SoldOutServant.net*.

Printed in Great Britain
by Amazon

22893524R00088